ADVICE FOR MONKS AND NUNS

Previously published by the LAMA YESHE WISDOM ARCHIVE

Becoming Your Own Therapist, by Lama Yeshe
Virtue and Reality, by Lama Zopa Rinpoche
Make Your Mind an Ocean, by Lama Yeshe
Teachings from the Vajrasattva Retreat, by Lama Zopa Rinpoche
Daily Purification: A Short Vajrasattva Meditation, by Lama Zopa Rinpoche
Making Life Meaningful, by Lama Zopa Rinpoche
The Essence of Tibetan Buddhism, by Lama Yeshe
Teachings from the Mani Retreat, by Lama Zopa Rinpoche
Direct and Unmistaken Method, by Lama Zopa Rinpoche

For initiates only
A Chat about Heruka, by Lama Zopa Rinpoche
A Chat about Yamantaka, by Lama Zopa Rinpoche

In association with TDL Publications
Mirror of Wisdom, by Geshe Tsultim Gyeltsen
Illuminating the Path, by His Holiness the Dalai Lama (forthcoming 2002)

*May whoever sees, touches, reads, remembers, or talks or thinks about these
booklets never be reborn in unfortunate circumstances, receive only rebirths
in situations conducive to the perfect practice of Dharma, meet only perfectly
qualified spiritual guides, quickly develop bodhicitta and immediately
attain enlightenment for the sake of all sentient beings.*

LAMA YESHE
LAMA ZOPA RINPOCHE

ADVICE FOR MONKS AND NUNS

Edited by Nicholas Ribush

Published by the LAMA YESHE WISDOM ARCHIVE for the
International Mahayana Institute

LAMA YESHE WISDOM ARCHIVE • BOSTON
www.LamaYeshe.com

A non-profit charitable organization for the benefit of
all sentient beings and a section of the Foundation for the
Preservation of the Mahayana Tradition
www.fpmt.org

First published 1998
1,000 copies for free distribution
Second printing 2002, 3,000 copies

LAMA YESHE WISDOM ARCHIVE
PO BOX 356
WESTON
MA 02493 USA

ISBN 1-891868-01-2

10 9 8 7 6 5 4 3 2

Front cover photograph by Carol Royce-Wilder
    (Lama Yeshe and Lama Zopa Rinpoche in California in 1975)
Book design by Mark Gatter

Printed in Canada on recycled, acid-free paper

Please contact the LAMA YESHE WISDOM ARCHIVE for copies of
our free booklets

CONTENTS

PUBLISHER'S ACKNOWLEDGMENTS

We are extremely grateful to our friends and supporters who have made it possible for the LAMA YESHE WISDOM ARCHIVE to both exist and function: to Lama Yeshe and Lama Zopa Rinpoche, whose kindness is impossible to repay; to Peter & Nicole Kedge and Venerable Ailsa Cameron for helping bring the ARCHIVE to its present state of development; to Venerable Roger Kunsang, Lama Zopa's tireless assistant, for his kindness and consideration; and to our sustaining supporters: Drs. Penny Noyce & Leo Liu, Barry & Connie Hershey, Joan Terry, Roger & Claire Ash-Wheeler, Claire Atkins, Richard Gere, Ecie Hursthouse, Lily Chang Wu, T. Y. Alexander, Therese Miller, Chris Dornan, Henry & Catherine Lau, Tom & Suzanne Castles, Datuk Tai Tsu Kuang, Chuah Kok Leng, the Caytons (Karuna, Pam, Bob & Amy), Tom Thorning, Tan Swee Eng, Salim Lee, Doren & Mary Harper, Claire Ritter, Sandra Magnussen, Cecily Drucker, Lynnea Elkind, Janet Moore, Su Hung, Carol Davies, Jack Morison, Dorian Ribush and Dharmawati Brechbuhl. We also thank most sincerely Massimo Corona and the FPMT International Office for their generous financial and administrative assistance.

We would like, as well, to express our appreciation for the kindness and compassion of all those generous benefactors mentioned in detail in our previous publications. They are too numerous to mention individually in this little book, but we value highly each and every contribution made to spreading the Dharma for the sake of the kind mother sentient beings.

Finally, we would also like to thank the many kind people who have asked that their donations be kept anonymous; the volunteers who have given so generously of their time to help us with our mailings, especially Therese Miller; our dedicated office staff, Jennifer Barlow and Angie Gittleman; Alison Ribush & Mandala Books (Melbourne) for much appreciated assistance with our work in Australia; and Dennis Heslop, Philip Bradley and our other friends at Wisdom Books (London) for their great help with our work in Europe.

If you, dear reader, would like to join this noble group of open-hearted altruists by contributing to the production of more free booklets by Lama Yeshe or Lama Zopa Rinpoche or to any other aspect of the LAMA YESHE WISDOM ARCHIVE's work, please contact us to find out how.

Through the merit of having contributed to the spread of the Buddha's teachings for the sake of all sentient beings, may our benefactors and their families and friends have long and healthy lives, all happiness, and may all their Dharma wishes be instantly fulfilled.

EDITOR'S INTRODUCTION

The LAMA YESHE WISDOM ARCHIVE is delighted to collaborate with the International Mahayana Institute in the production of this small collection of talks by Lama Yeshe and Lama Zopa Rinpoche to their ordained students, the monks and nuns of the Foundation for the Preservation of the Mahayana Tradition. We hope to publish more of these talks in future.

The first talk was given by Lama Yeshe at Kopan Monastery in December, 1973, to a small group of Western students a few weeks prior to their ordination. This was the beginning of the IMI. The second talk was given at Tushita Retreat Centre, Dharamsala, over two nights in April, 1982, during the first Enlightened Experience Celebration. Essentially, this was the beginning of Nalanda Monastery.

The last two talks were given by Lama Zopa Rinpoche quite recently. The first was actually an essay prepared for publication in *Mandala* magazine in 1996; the second was given during teachings at Vajrapani Institute, California, in 1997.

The continued existence of the Buddhadharma depends upon the continued existence of the Sangha—the community of ordained practitioners, monks and nuns—one of the three Buddhist Refuges. In these talks, Lama Yeshe and Lama Zopa Rinpoche explain the great benefits of practicing Dharma as an ordained person, how to keep the ordination pure, the purpose of the monastic community, how to live together as monks and nuns and much more. The necessity for the lay community to support the Sangha is also made clear, and not only monks and nuns but lay practitioners, too, will gain much by reading this book.

I thank Ven. Connie Miller, Rand Engel and Wendy Cook for their editorial suggestions, which greatly improved the readability of these talks, and Mark Gatter for so kindly designing this book.

May the Sangha flourish in the ten directions for the benefit of all sentient beings.

THE FIRST TALK

Around the time of the fifth Kopan meditation course, in November 1973, ten Western Dharma students had asked Lama Yeshe's permission to get ordained. Lama suggested that they take their ordinations the following January, in Bodhgaya, after His Holiness the Dalai Lama had given the Kalachakra initiation. In December 1973, Lama gathered into his room these ten prospective monks and nuns, together with five or six of his students who had already been ordained, and offered the following advice. This was the first talk Lama ever gave to his Sangha community.

Today I want to express my feelings to my sisters and brothers, because what we're seeing here is a very remarkable, revolutionary explosion of energy. But this is an internal revolution, not an external one. It has given me a lot to think about, but a very, very good feeling as well.

I feel some kind of intuitive responsibility for the decision you've made to live in the Dharma. Therefore, I've thought a lot about how you can integrate your lives with Dharma so that you can continue to experience this internal revolutionary energy without interruption and develop your minds to their unlimited potential.

My feeling is that it would be much better if the Sangha were to stay together, communicating with each other, rather than people getting ordained and then going off on their own. If you do go off on your own, worldly conditions will make your life difficult; it will be much harder for you to practice Dharma.

For example, when Sangha are here at Kopan, we help them lead a monastic life. There are always lamas present and, as a result, our students get some kind of energy that helps them control their minds and makes it easier for them to keep their ordination. If, instead, they run off and stay in some other place where the conditions are not so good, their lives become very difficult. If, on top of that, they get sick, this confluence of internal and external problems makes their lives even more difficult.

As you know, just because you're a monk or nun does not mean that you've reached enlightenment. It simply means that you have gained an understanding of the nature of samsara and have decided to work continuously to develop within yourself the everlasting, peaceful path of liberation. That's all. Getting ordained doesn't give you immediate control over your mind; it doesn't mean you are completely liberated. It's not like that.

Our minds are uncontrolled. We need to control them. Monastic life allows us to develop our minds in a very comfortable way until we have truly achieved complete control over them and have gained such great knowledge-wisdom that even should we go to some berserk place, we are able to control that berserk energy instead of its controlling us.

For us beginners, the desire to attain everlasting peaceful liberation is just like a flower seed. A flower seed needs to be cared for, watered, kept warm, fertilized—many things are necessary. Water alone is not enough; it needs fertilizer. Similarly, we need Dharma teachings. If we get teachings and retreat, we can wake up fantastically; enthusiastic energy always comes. Otherwise, we're like flowers that have been given only a few drops of water; when problems arise, we will find it difficult to deal with them. Our minds are just like flowers; we have to take good care of them.

In Tibet, lay people looked after the Sangha. They had great respect for the Sangha because they knew that despite experiencing difficult conditions, the Sangha did their duty. By "difficult conditions" I don't mean that people were beating them. Their deluded minds beat them; their deluded minds didn't like fighting against wisdom. Lay people knew that Sangha life was difficult, but worthwhile, so they respected the Sangha's internal knowledge, their control. Therefore, the Sangha had much support in Tibet.

For us, it's not like that. We have to take more responsibility for ourselves. Wherever our Western Sangha live, even in India or Nepal, it's not that different from the West. I mean, even in the East, you eat Western food—you can't live like Indians or Nepalis. Therefore, we need somehow to put our Western lifestyle and Dharma together. You need coffee; have coffee. You need sweet tea, have sweet tea; you need medicine, take medicine; you need cake, maybe eat cake! You have certain habits, you have a particular heritage and your bodies have been raised in a certain way.

We can't tell you to eat only tsampa, drink only Tibetan tea, that's all you can have. We cannot force you like that. And you don't need such external changes; you don't need to be focused on cutting out various kinds of food, giving up things that you're used to. Really, it's not necessary. It's more important to provide your body with what it's used to, with what it needs to stay healthy. That's more important than, "Oh, I'm a renunciate—I should renounce this, I should give up that." It's not like that. Renunciation should be more in the mind than on the physical level. "I want to give up my wallet! Please, somebody take it!" That just makes things more difficult, dear. OK. I think you people understand this.

As I mentioned, I feel what's happening here is remarkable, and I've been thinking about it, thinking about this remarkable energy and how to keep it going. So I worry a little...well, when I say I worry, I don't mean I'm suffering. Perhaps concern is a better word— I'm very concerned. Therefore, I think we need some rules. Of course, we have our thirty-six precepts, but in addition to those we have other rules: government rules, monastery rules, meditation course rules.

For example, during the course you have to get up at a certain time, have meals at certain times, do this, do that. Those rules are not contained in the thirty-six precepts, are they? But still, they are necessary if you are living in a certain situation. We make those kinds of rules, don't we? You can't reject them: "Who made these rules? Why should I get up at 5:30 in the morning and have coffee? Who says? Lord Buddha never said that." Well, it doesn't matter whether Lord Buddha said those words or not; such rules are necessary for a communal way of life.

We have to introduce some kind of small discipline when creating a Sangha community. For example, when you become a monk or nun, you're not allowed to stay in situations that are too samsaric, such as places where there's a lot of dancing and drinking. It's very dangerous if you frequent such places. Bringing your deluded mind to samsaric places is like bringing a piece of paper close to a fire. [Here Lama brings a piece of paper closer and closer to the candle on his table until it bursts into flames.] You're OK at a distance, but if you get too close to fire, you'll get burned. Flammable materials should be kept away from fire, and we beginners should stay away from dangerous situations.

As I said before, when you become a monk or nun, it doesn't mean that you are liberated or enlightened. It simply means that you have decided to act in such a way that you can eventually reach perfect control, liberation, freedom—there are so many words, it doesn't matter which you use. Somehow, you are searching for that. You get ordained because you understand there's a better way of finding joy in life. That is why we make these kinds of rules for the Sangha.

Take Boudhanath, for example. Boudhanath is a holy place, but many people, especially Nepalese and Tibetans, also consider it a drinking place, a place where men and women get together for fun. They make chang [Tibetan beer] there. I don't really know if this is true or not, but this is what people say. There are probably places like that in Kathmandu as well. Actually, you people know this better than I do. When I try to explain samsara, you're probably thinking, "What's this lama talking about? I can describe this much better than he can." I'm joking!

Anyway, if a monk stays in this kind of place, his Sangha friends should say, "Dear, why are you living in that terrible situation? You know you're not allowed to stay there. Wouldn't it be better if you came and stayed in a quieter place? Since you are Sangha, surely you'd be better off in the monastery."

When Sangha leave here and go home, those who remain should

keep in touch with them, so that even while they're away, they still feel close to their Dharma brothers and sisters. Otherwise, they might start thinking, "Oh, now I'm alone, I can do whatever I like. Before I was in my guru's Sangha community, but now that I'm back in my own country, I'm free." You can feel the possibility of this happening, can't you? I'm not just being negative; the possibility is there, dear, OK? Therefore, we need to develop strong togetherness energy instead of allowing the Sangha to split up and go their own way.

I think we should create a community specifically for Western Sangha. But don't think I'm just talking about the fifteen of you in this room. You can imagine what's going to happen. Now we have this many Sangha; after the next meditation course there will be more. Then after the next one, more again. After some time we might become 100,000 strong! It's possible. I mean, Dharma wisdom is there, isn't it? It's possible. Therefore, we need somehow to develop strong togetherness, and in that way we'll be able to practice Dharma easily, without being overwhelmed by agitated worldly conditions.

A simple example: a few Sangha come up to Kopan. We don't have good conditions here, so they feel uncomfortable and leave feeling negative, thinking, "It's not possible to stay at the monastery. I'll have to find a home for myself to lead my own samsaric life." It's possible. Our minds react to such tiny causes. Therefore, we have to discuss how to face the world, how to integrate Dharma into our way of life.

If monks and nuns have difficulty just keeping their physical lives together, how will they ever get the chance to study and retreat? The strength of the Sangha community is that it ensures that everybody has a chance to take teachings and retreat; it makes sure that everybody is OK and minimizes the external conditions that cause one to lose mental discipline. I think this is really worthwhile. It helps a lot. There's a Sangha vibration, you see; when you look at each other, there's a vibration that automatically helps you control your energy. You should check this for yourselves.

If you stay in a place where everybody is drinking, for example, at first you kind of intellectualize, "They're like that; I'm like this." It might be OK for a while, but I'm not talking about what happens at an intellectual level. Subconsciously, at the level of intuitive feeling, something else is going on, and sooner or later, *poof!* Just as paper catches fire when it gets too close to a flame, you get completely caught up in whatever's going on around you. As I always say, the mind is just like a mirror. It automatically reflects whatever's in front of it. Intellectually, your mind is saying, "Oh, that's samsara," but whatever you come into contact with leaves an imprint on your mind. So, the day comes when you're a little bit tired, a little bit thirsty, so you have a little drink—a little, little drink. "Hmmm, that was good. I was a little thirsty and I had a little drink. No harm done." But that's just the start. You know how children are with candy. They eat one: "Wow! That was good." Then they want more...and more...and more...and more...like that. Well, you people know. I'm just giving an example. You know how the mind works in this kind of situation as well as I do.

The conditions in which you put yourself are very, very important. Lay people's way of life and the Sangha way of life are different. You should discriminate somehow, shouldn't you? I'm not just pointing negatively, "Oh, that's bad." Lay people's lifestyle is their own trip, but our way of life is something else; our way of life is the thirty-six precepts. You have to discriminate. If you don't, then you're no better than a crazy person. Crazy people can't tell the difference between good and bad. We have to be able to make the distinction. For example, a butcher's job is to kill, but our job is different, isn't it? The butcher's way of life and the Sangha way of life should be different, shouldn't they? If someone then accuses me of discriminating, I'm going to say, "Yes! I'm discriminating." As long as you haven't transcended discrimination, you should discriminate. Of course, you can argue with words in many different ways, but ultimately, words don't mean anything. We need discriminating wisdom.

Anyway, all this is just my own opinion, my own feeling. Nobody told me to tell you all this; nor is it an ego game. I just felt that since your Dharma understanding has led you to the conclusion that you want to get ordained, I should express my feelings about the way things are developing. Western people aren't stupid; they can check up, they can see. If you as Western monks and nuns have a good attitude, behave well and develop a strong Sangha community with group togetherness, Western people will respect you. They'll feel that Westerners becoming Sangha is worthwhile. They might even want to help you.

So, the conclusion is that you can choose your own way of life, irrespective of what other people in your country or your society do. We have a choice. We can look at things with wisdom; we can check up. For example, we come here to Kopan and create our own conditions. It has nothing to do with the Nepalese government. They don't tell us what to do. We ourselves make sure we have teachings, make sure everybody is OK, make sure we work together to achieve our aims. Accordingly, we create our own world. With the right conditions, it becomes easy for us to do what we want to do. That's all.

Now that I've expressed my feelings, you should discuss amongst yourselves how to create strong Sangha togetherness. Don't think I'm attached to keeping you at Kopan. Don't think that I'm hung up on that. It doesn't matter to me where you live, as long as you maintain strong Sangha togetherness. You should create those kinds of conditions. Think with wisdom and be strong.

THE ADVANTAGES OF MONASTIC LIFE:
PART ONE

In 1982, Lama Yeshe organized the first Enlightened Experience Celebration, a five-month series of teachings, initiations and retreats held in Bodhgaya and Dharamsala, India. About one hundred International Mahayana Institute monks and nuns attended. During the Dharamsala part of the program, Lama Yeshe called the monks and nuns into the gompa at Tushita Retreat Centre and, over two successive evenings (April 17 & 18), gave the following talks.

I want to say a few words to the Western monks and nuns gathered here today.

Somehow, we are very fortunate. Trying to live according to Lord Buddha's vinaya rules as best we can, even for a day or a month, we are extremely fortunate. It's good enough.

These days, the world is degenerating rapidly into impurity, aggression and the grasping at resources, leading people into a state of tremendous anxiety. Though we are monks and nuns, we cannot ignore what is happening in the world. Newspapers and magazines are full of this information; even way up here in the mountains, we can feel that negative vibration.

Therefore, we have good reason to be proud of our ordination. We should be proud, rather than thinking, "I'm a monk—I'm so useless, so lonely"; "I'm a nun—I'm so useless, so lonely." Instead of repeating that mantra, feel proud of what you are.

Also, I'm very satisfied with the way this Dharma Celebration we're holding has gone. When you consider that most 20th century Westerners are living simply to grasp at sense pleasures, it is like a dream that more than one hundred Western monks and nuns can come together at an event like this. Remember how His Holiness Ling Rinpoche told us in Bodhgaya that although tourists had been going there for a long time, our gathering was an historic occasion; never before had Westerners come there together to live and practice according to the Buddhist way of life. So, we are very, very fortunate. You should be very happy. Living purely by the vinaya rules even for a day is very rare; your doing so is good enough for me.

HOW AND WHY THE IMI STARTED

I'd like to recount a little of the history of the International Mahayana Institute [IMI]. Some people had doubts when I called this organization the "International Mahayana Institute": they didn't like the name. I don't care! Who cares whether some like it and others don't— that's just the dualistic mind at work. Without an object of hatred, there's no desire. But I came up with this name because the words mean something. The members of our Sangha come from all over the world, so we are truly international; the Buddhism we practice is Mahayana; and since we're an educational phenomenon, I called it an institute: International Mahayana Institute.

Why form such an institute? Why shouldn't our international monks and nuns just go to the mountains and live like Milarepa?

Why do we need an organization? Well, take this Dharma Celebration, for example: how many people did it take to organize it? Without organization, how could this Enlightened Experience Celebration have happened? That's my answer. Even two people living together as a couple need to organize their lives. We do need organization. Some hippies reject organization—that is stupid; they don't understand. They can't organize even their own lives let alone do something that benefits so many others.

So why did I create this institute? Because I felt that according to the vinaya rules, it was my responsibility to do so. Our Sangha members started their Dharma studies with lam-rim; this gave them some understanding of the nature of samsara, the benefits of renunciation and the best way to practice. Through their own experience they were enthusiastic about getting ordained. So I said yes. But, you know, for me to say yes is easy; I can ordain anybody any day just by reciting the words of the ordination ceremony, "Blah, blah, blah." But ordaining someone is more than just a day's work. Lord Buddha said that you have to take care of your Sangha. But how do you take care of the Sangha? I'm just a stupid Himalayan monk with neither worldly nor organizational experience. I was never even a manager in Sera Monastery. I was just a simple monk. All I did was study and serve and cook for my teacher. When I checked out what needed to be done, it appeared difficult for me to take responsibility for what has now become almost one hundred monks and nuns. This process led me to conclude that if I created a Sangha community organization, its members would help each other.

We need security. We're what Tibetans call "white crows." Tibetans consider that Westerners becoming monks and nuns is as impossible as a crow's being white. As far as society is concerned, we're outcasts. Our pink faces show that we're not part of Tibetan society, and because of our renounced attitude, we're outcasts from Western society as well. They think we're Hare Krishnas. Not that I'm putting Hare Krishnas down, but people reject us because that's what they think we are. So I felt that we needed the security of creating our own category so that we could exercise our own reality. Therefore, about eight years ago I formed this organization.

Since then we've been growing by about five or ten monks and nuns a year. We originally established the organization in Kathmandu, at Kopan, and in my view the monks and nuns who stayed there were successful. They studied lam-rim; they learned some rituals. But after some time the government changed the visa laws so that it became impossibly expensive for them to stay. So I thought, well, that's OK; it's no big deal. They are Westerners, not Nepalis; it would be stupid for them to think of spending their entire lives in Nepal, in the Third World. Still, they had renounced the comfort of this life, which is a very good thing. So, I thought deeply about what to do.

It took a long time to establish Nalanda, our first Western monastery. It wasn't easy. In the West you have to get involved with dollars. Without money, you can't buy land. Fortunately, one devoted student offered us the property in Lavaur, so finally we now have a place that offers us the opportunity to lead a monastic life and take care of each other. We do need that.

We have renounced comfort to a certain extent, but we still have our problems; we have not yet eliminated the three poisons. We're not buddhas; we're not arhats. We need to take care of each other emotionally. It's difficult for lay people to do this for us. If monks cry, lay people don't understand: "This monk is supposed to have renounced samsara, now he's crying for it?" But other monks and nuns do understand and can comfort each other, can be warm to each other: "Oh, don't cry. Yes, today's a little cloudy, but it will clear up tomorrow."

There are many differences between lay people and those who are ordained. Their lifestyles are different; their thinking is different; their responsibilities are different. But up until now, just a few of the older monks and nuns have been dedicated to organizing food, clothing, shelter, transport between Nepal and India, and retreat and teaching facilities in order to keep our Sangha community together. Newer monks and nuns can't appreciate how hard we have worked; the old ones know. We have tried our best; we have a long history.

We reached a certain point where there were so many of us without income that it was almost impossible to go on. Still, we tried to take care of everybody. Some Sangha had their own money and they shared it with others. I was very happy to see them doing that. But these days we're scattered all over the world; we don't have our own home, so economically it's difficult to share our limited resources to help each other. In the future, when Nalanda Monastery is more firmly established, I hope that everybody will share in order to help each other.

I cannot organize all this myself. I have a vision of what needs to be done, but I can't take a needle and thread and sew all your robes myself; I cannot do all these everyday tasks. You people need to get organized to help each other. This is very necessary. You see, monks and nuns need education. How can we offer them a good education if we don't get organized? You can see how difficult it will be.

Anyway, that's a short history of how we started.

WHAT IT MEANS TO BE A MONK OR NUN

Let's talk about how, at the beginning, you should become a monk or nun, or what it means to be a monk or nun. Permitting Westerners to become monks and nuns is not a job to take lightly. Nor is it good to ordain people too easily. We have learned a lot from the experience of the past eight years.

First of all, if your parents are still your guardians or if you have a good relationship with them, you need their permission to become a monk or nun. They should be happy about your decision. This is important; we've had some experience with this. Some people got ordained without their parents' permission, but then later, their negative mind arose. You know, the negative mind, the ego, always likes to rationalize—"Well now, my mother never really liked me being ordained, so I think I'd better give back my robes for her sake."

I know. I've had this experience. I say, "OK, good." I am not that stupid. If you really want to keep your ordination, who cares what your samsaric mother thinks? Your samsaric mother is stupid, too; full of ignorance, full of desire, full of hatred. Who cares? Lord Buddha himself said that if you are not strong, if you are weak, you need your parents' permission, but if you are totally convinced that what you are doing is right, then you don't. I tell you, our parents are just as stupid as we are. We call our country of birth "the nest of samsara."

It's true. I look at my own situation. When I lived in Tibet, my uncle took care of me. Parents mean well, but giving you food, clothes and money with samsaric mind, worrying about your reputation—I'm sorry, it's not sufficient. So, what I am saying is, if you are strong enough, you don't need your parents' permission. Shakyamuni

Buddha is a good example. Who gave him permission to leave home, to leave his kingdom? Nobody. He had hundreds of wives grasping at him; there's no way they would have given him permission to go lead an ascetic life.

Many Westerners want to become monks or nuns simply because, "I hate society; I hate my parents' way of life—there's no alternative, I have to do it. Anyway, it seems that monks and nuns have an easy life, so I think I'll get ordained." That is wrong. Lord Buddha said it's wrong to become a monk or nun just to simplify your life in the sense that you don't have to worry about getting food or clothing or worry about some husband or wife. That is not the connotation of the pratimoksha. Prati means individual; moksha means liberation, or nirvana. It implies that we should understand our own personal samsaric situation and feel dissatisfied with that, not with the external object of society. If this understanding really touches your heart and you become a monk or nun on this basis, your ordination is a truly renounced one.

I tell you, if you become a monk or nun out of bad motivation, you will never succeed. Correct motivation is the most important thing.

WHY DID YOU GET ORDAINED?

The way you get ordained, though, is good, in that you are old enough to decide for yourselves. Westerners becoming monks and nuns after the age of twenty is better than the way we Tibetans do it. I was just a stupid six-year-old boy when I decided to become a monk. Not so smart; I lost the chance to enjoy many of life's experiences! All of you have seen the sense world, you've had enough male-female relationships, you've experienced most of what worldly life has to offer and you've reached a certain point where you think, "I want to make my life more easygoing instead of always being in conflict with others and hurting them in human relationships." This is actually a better, more Dharma way of getting ordained.

The Tibetan way is sometimes culturally determined. Of course, Tibetan culture has its good aspects and its bad; I can't say all Tibetan culture is good. It also encourages development of the samsaric, egotistical mind. Therefore, it is the responsibility of your preceptor—lama, geshe, yogi, yogini, whatever—to ensure that in your heart you have the right motivation for getting ordained.

Sometimes people are driven by neurotic, emotional feelings: "Oh, the lam-rim says that renunciation is the best way to practice! Hey, let's go! I want to be just like Milarepa!" This often happened in Tibet. It was common—many of us were like that. For example, monks from the colleges would go to hear some high lama teach lam-rim, where he would explain how fantastic Milarepa was or how Lama Tsong Khapa renounced the world. Many of them would then run off from college and go up into the mountains to lead ascetic lives. But of course, after a few days, most of them would come back down! That's just emotional.

Westerners, too, get excited: "Oh, becoming a monk, becoming a nun, what a good idea!" Becoming a monk or nun is not simply a good idea! Actually, the life of a monk or nun is quite difficult. Lay people should have compassion for us! It's true! Tibetan lay people have compassion for the Sangha, or at least, they used to—I'm not sure if they still do. Perhaps these days they have given up on monks and nuns. Anyway, just having an emotional feeling is not enough.

Pratimoksha means renounced ordination. Renunciation means that somehow you have the strength to really comprehend that all worldly pleasures, whatever they are, are not for you. If you feel that something totally incompatible with Sangha behavior is actually wonderful, your life as a monk or nun will be very difficult indeed. If, however, you have a good understanding of the universal samsaric situation, true renunciation will come to you very easily. Therefore, before getting ordained, you should receive perfect, detailed explanations of the nature of samsara and liberation and what renunciation really means. Attitude makes a big difference—a big difference. When you have a renounced attitude, all your superstitious tendencies are somehow dispelled. Psychologically, having no more expectations makes all the difference.

Sometimes I tell people wanting to get ordained to wait for a couple of years. I think this is good. Live as a monk or nun for a while and then we can see about ordaining you. Some people have criticized me for this, but what to do? I think it's important for some people to live as monks or nuns for a couple of years without carrying the heavy burden of ordination. Some have done this and after two years have still wanted to become monks and nuns. This is fantastic. There is some significance.

I have also told some people to renounce worldly life, wear robes and live as Sangha. In Tibetan we call this *nyam-par nam-sum*: live as a monk or nun, listen to the abbot's advice and don't behave loosely, like lay people do—these three. It is so easy; we have these three simple conditions. You live like that for a while, until you reach the point where you are sure that this is the way you want to live the rest of your life. Then you can take the actual thirty-six novice vows. This is an easy way to develop a good understanding of what it's like to be ordained: there's no pressure; you have nothing to lose; it's flexible. I think this is a good idea. In summary, one should not become a monk or nun too easily.

Then, when you become ordained, it is very important for you to receive a detailed explanation of the vows.

THE RELATIONSHIP WITH YOUR ABBOT

What about your relationship with your abbot? According to the vinaya, the person who ordains you becomes your abbot. He becomes responsible for you in the way that a father is responsible for the welfare of his daughter or son; it's that kind of relationship. Do you remember what was explained to you when you were ordained? It's important; it's no joke. As I said before, giving ordination is easy: "Blah, blah, blah...OK, now you're a monk or nun, goodbye!" One hour and it's all over. That's easy. But Lord Buddha said, "No! You have to maintain a strong relationship with your abbot. Whatever important question comes up, I want you to ask him if it's right or wrong." That way you take care of each other.

These days, somehow it's difficult for 20th century monks and nuns to sustain a strong relationship with their abbots. They split with their parents, they split with their gurus, they split with their abbot...some kind of revolutionary lifestyle. Older monks, however, know that being close to their vinaya abbot has great significance, that it really means something, that it is very important.

Don't think, "I'm an individualist, I can do what I like." Yes, you can do whatever you like. Nobody's pushing you, but if you make a commitment, if you choose a lifestyle that has certain goals, you need many interdependent phenomena to develop in that direction, to help you reach that point.

The Western lifestyle gives you great freedom but it also encourages you to develop a strong individualistic ego. So generally, you just do whatever your ego says, and if you don't, you feel frustrated. You have to change that attitude.

When you get ordained, you have to trust that your abbot can give you energy, guide you, help you. You should have confidence that your abbot won't give you bad advice and lead you into some disastrous situation. Therefore, you should build a good connection with your abbot based on the right understanding that he can help you until you are liberated. Don't be ruled by your strong individualistic ego. Instead, develop a good relationship with your teacher and your Dharma brothers and sisters. They are the resources from which your Dharma wisdom grows.

WHAT TO DO AFTER YOU'VE BEEN ORDAINED

After ordination, you must act according to the vinaya rules as much as you possibly can. That is your responsibility. Getting ordained is easy; it takes less than a day. The difficulty lies in keeping going; that's where the hardships are.

You need to study the vinaya rules in detail. For example, as you may remember, the act of killing has four branches: motivation, object, action and completion. To completely break the vow of not killing, all four branches need to be involved. Even if you do something that breaks a vow, if one of these four aspects is missing from the action, you are not completely negative; the vow has been only partially broken.

It is important to know these things. Many times Westerners come to me crying that they've lost their ordination. But when I check up, they haven't lost it. They may have broken something—this is my experience—they may have broken a vow in a small way, but they have not broken it completely. Vows are broken by degrees. You have to study these things clean clear—then you know how to keep your ordination.

Since we are beginners, we sometimes break vows, but there's a way to confess such transgressions. There are also degrees of confession and different ways of confessing. Usually we conduct formal confession ceremonies [*so-jong*] twice a month. It's good to attend those. Participating in so-jong is enough to purify the great accumulation of negativity that comes from breaking precepts.

VINAYA RULES CAN CHANGE

Remember that vinaya rules can change with the times. As our culture changes, the vinaya rules themselves can also change. Lord Buddha himself said this. But that doesn't mean that these days you can kill—it doesn't mean that. Study the vinaya in detail.

For example, Western women's use of perfume is commonplace; it's nothing special, no big deal. But in Tibet and other Third World countries, when a woman puts on perfume, it is something special—people think that there's something going on in her mind. In the West, it's nothing: both men and women use perfume. It's almost obligatory! So you have to take such cultural differences into account too.

REINFORCING YOUR ORDINATION WITH MEDITATION

You have to understand the vows more deeply than just being able to enumerate them. In my opinion, keeping vows in a monastery in the East is easy. But in the West, even knowing intellectually clean clear all the details of the vows is not enough. Westerners need to reinforce their intellectual understanding with meditation. Otherwise, it is impossible for them to keep their ordination. The environment is too overwhelming. It's telling you, "Do this, do that; if you don't, you're stupid. If you don't grasp at Coca-Cola, you're stupid." I'm exaggerating a little, but the impact of these influences is so strong, so strong. I really feel grateful that there are some Westerners who are trying to keep their ordinations pure. To live in the West and do this you have to be strong inside. Otherwise, it's not possible.

In the West, some people think you're almost a criminal if you're ordained: "The man next door is very strange. He lives alone, no wife or children. He must be sick." That is the popular understanding, the reality of your culture. As a result, Westerners need to expend tremendous energy to keep their ordinations. Life in the West is not easy. That's why it is not an easy job for Tibetan monks to go to the West either.

Of course, we have centers all over the world, and if you live in one, it's almost like living in a monastery. That's different. In that small world you may be able to preserve your ordination. But where it gets difficult is when you go out from the center.

Therefore, as monks and nuns you should put as much energy as you can into meditating every day. This will generate some internal satisfaction and enable you to avoid the stress of breaking vows. Without meditation, it's just not possible.

CREATING A CONDUCIVE ENVIRONMENT

One's environment must be conducive. We put a lot of energy into protecting our monks and nuns, into helping them keep their ordination. We do; we really do. In our centers, we try to create separate quarters for the Sangha. We have tried in many different ways, but so far it has often been economically unfeasible. But now, with the creation of Nalanda Monastery, I hope we'll be able to live the monastic life we desire and thereby be able to develop our internal world quickly. So really, I strongly advise all of you to live the monastic life as much as you possibly can, until you have the internal strength to withstand the pressures of the outside world. Otherwise, it will be very, very difficult.

Remember what Vasubandhu said in his Abhidharmakosha? One of the factors that cause delusions to explode within you is the object: the object makes you deluded. Your mind is like a mirror—it reflects objects, superstitions are produced and delusions arise, resulting in deluded actions. Therefore, the environment is very important. So we should do something about it now. I would like all of you, for the benefit of the majority, for yourselves and others, to live a monastic life. You should give priority to that; it is so worthwhile. Of course, we each have different skills—some people can do things others can't—so there can be exceptions. For example, some may be able to lead an ascetic life in retreat; that would be an exception.

At the very least, monks and nuns should receive a basic education; in other words, teachings on the lam-rim. Without the lam-rim, monks and nuns will be disasters. You need to practice lam-rim meditation in order to grow. However, in the West, where people can be so intellectual, knowing the lam-rim alone may not be enough. You also need to understand the philosophical basis of your Dharma knowledge in order to prove your points with reasoning and logic.

MONASTIC RULES

Besides following the vinaya rules, you must also observe the internal rules of the monastery. These are related to the vinaya but are not vows as such. For example, if you don't attend morning puja, you may not be breaking a vow but you're breaking a Sangha community rule, so it's not so good. If you are sick, or if you have lung, an exception can be made. You can go to the gekyö and explain that you are not well and ask permission to skip the puja. Lord Buddha always took care of the sick; that's an exception. But if you don't have lung or some physical illness, not participating is very bad, very bad. Actually, I tell you, it means you have no compassion.

Look at thangkas of what we call the *rig-sum gom-po* [Avalokiteshvara, Manjushri and Vajrapani]: sometimes Avalokiteshvara is in the center and below him, like servants or disciples, are Manjushri and Vajrapani. In other representations you'll see Manjushri or Vajrapani in the middle and the other two below. This has great significance. Manjushri is the embodiment of enlightened wisdom, but sometimes he acts as Avalokiteshvara's disciple. He doesn't do this for his own benefit but for that of others. We should be prepared to do the same thing.

Shakyamuni Buddha himself is another good example of what I'm saying. When he came into this world as the son of a king, he was already enlightened. He didn't need the worldly hassles of samsaric royalty and hundreds of wives. Do you think he needed all that hassle? No, of course he didn't. He was beyond hassles, but nevertheless, he manifested in that way for the benefit of others.

Similarly, even if you have supreme knowledge of sutra and tantra, even if you're an arya being or even Manjushri himself, in order to benefit the Sangha community, for the good of the majority, you should participate in their activities as much as you can. If you are busy with some Dharma work or are sick, as I mentioned before, an exception can be made; just ask permission. In that case, you should not feel guilty. Everybody will understand.

Theoretically, I should tell you that monks and nuns should get up early in the morning, but I can't really push you on this because I don't get up early myself! I'm a bad example! Well, it depends on what time you go to bed. My nature is not to go to bed early, so I get up late. I'm a bad example, so don't follow me. It's not so good, but I learned it from you people! But really, I strongly encourage you to go to bed early and get up early. Don't go to bed at 12:30 or 1:00 in the morning; 10:00 or 11:00 p.m., certainly before midnight, is much better. Then you can get up at 5:30 or 6:00 in the morning and do your practice, pray and meditate.

Many of my Sangha seem to be just like Tibetans, although I don't really know where this Tibetan trip comes from. It's not my trip; I don't know who set that example. They don't do their prayers and commitments in the morning; they just hang about distractedly all day. Then at midnight, they suddenly freak out, pull out their books and finally get down to doing their commitments. They put their pechas on their knees in front of them, but as soon as they start reciting, they nod off. Then they wake up and continue for a while until they fall asleep again. Then they wake up again and find their book on the floor, so they have to start over. It takes a couple of hours just to do three pages! Then it's 3:00 a.m. and they do a few more lines and fall asleep once again. It goes on like this until the sun comes up. Then they just give up and go to sleep until lunchtime. That Tibetan trip is not so good. I don't know who taught them that. It's better to sleep soundly; sleep helps you. At least at that time your mind is tranquil and peaceful because your gross mind is absorbed. Then you awaken clean clear, physically and mentally rested and healthy.

I am saying that when you do your prayers, you should do them with full concentration and good motivation instead of just reciting your mantras mindlessly, "Blah, blah, blah...OK, finished!" Then your sleep becomes so comfortable, so clean clear. This is much better than the other way.

Each day of your life is important. Your entire life is made up of these days, one after another. Therefore, you should organize your life: "When I get up I'm going to do this, then next I'll do this, then this, this, this...." You should organize yourself. Then your life becomes useful and you don't waste your time.

If you make a program for your life, you'll see clearly how you waste your time. For example, the two hours you spend talking nonsense with your friends benefits neither yourself nor others. If you don't make a program, you don't realize how much time you are wasting. So, make a general program and within that, a more detailed schedule. It's up to you; you can be flexible. But somehow, you should organize every day of your life. It's very useful. When you do this, you should also make sure that you balance your activities: your intellect, your emotions and your practical application.

Organizing a balanced day is very important. If you don't put one day together, then two days are not together, one month is not together, one year is not together, and you finish up wasting your entire life. That's why we need to organize our lives. And that's where the monastery comes in. You don't realize it yet, but monastic life gives us a schedule for our daily lives. We should be very grateful for that, I tell you. When I went to the monastery, the rules made me get myself together in a way that I could never have done alone. Monasteries are very, very useful.

You can't imagine how much we human beings can accomplish; it's unbelievable. We can do so much but sometimes are unaware of our own ability. When you put yourself into a situation that brings out the best in you, you can surprise yourself: "Incredible! I can do that!" After you've been in such a situation for some time, when you look back at what you have done, you feel so good, very proud of yourself. If you check what happens when you're in a place where there are no rules, you can see what a disastrous effect it has on your mind. That gives you a new appreciation of monastic discipline.

Monastic rules are very important, extremely important. For example, now, here, at this Dharma Celebration, you monks and nuns are living a monastic life: how do you feel? Is it beneficial or not? Do you feel that your attitude has changed or not? Has it made your life easier? I think the answer to these questions is, yes. It is definitely true: we are supporting each other. And that's exactly what the lam-rim teaches: all our knowledge, our reputation, our goodness comes from mother sentient beings, from other people. You can see that this is scientifically true. It's not some kind of metaphysical gobbledygook. It is so important for us to support each other.

You should, however, expect to find some rules in the monastery that were not laid down by Lord Buddha himself. These are necessary because of the local environment. You should accept them, instead of negating them, "Oh, Lord Buddha never made that rule. Why do you say I can't do that?"

First of all, without realizing it, you have already accepted in principle the existence of such rules. For example, the long Tibetan zen that we wear. Lord Buddha didn't say anything about monks wearing long zens, but you accept them automatically. Long zens are from Tibetan culture. Lord Buddha explained in detail how the teaching robe, the chö-gö, should be, but I never saw anything in the vinaya about long zens. But you just blindly accept them. You blindly accept certain things just because Tibetan people do them. That's stupid. However, monastic rules make sense. They help you grow, and that is their only purpose. Otherwise, why would we make them? There would be no point.

Who is responsible for seeing that these rules are observed? Does everybody have authority? Can just anyone say, "Blah, blah, blah...."? No. It is the abbot and the gekyö who have the authority to enforce the monastic rules. Therefore, when you go to a monastery you should accept that "The abbot and the gekyö are my dear friends, my spiritual friends, my leaders." You should have that attitude, that motivation, rather than think, "I'm Spanish, he's American. Why should I listen to him?" or "I'm Italian, that Tibetan monk doesn't eat pizza. Why should I take any notice of what he says? He can't offer me pizza or mozzarella." You should change that attitude. He is kind; he works hard. It is not easy being the leader; you should have compassion for him.

The leaders are trying to help you, even though they may be experiencing many difficulties themselves. Don't think that they're on power trips when they tell you this or that. Understand that the rules are there to benefit the majority. You are just one person. If you break the rules, you are damaging what benefits the majority; you are harming other sentient beings. Don't think that to harm others you have to stab them with a knife or do something flagrant like that. Destroying what benefits the majority of the community means you are harming them. Ignorance is like that; it sees only "my benefit."

PUTTING UP WITH DIFFICULTIES

You people have no idea what monastic life was like in Tibet; it was really hard. By comparison, your life here is almost a god-realm existence—even though you find something to complain about almost every day: "There's no running water...blah, blah, blah...we don't have comfortable beds...." Go down to the village and see how the poor Indian people live, how they just put up their simple cots and sleep in the street. In Tibetan monasteries, the monks would sometimes have to sit up all night on the cold ground in winter. When it was necessary, we underwent many hardships. It's not that we'd create all these hardships on purpose, just for the sake of putting up with them; that would be stupid. But when there's some benefit, you should be prepared to struggle and it should not bother you.

You should have the attitude, "As long as it contributes to my growth and benefits all mother sentient beings, I'll put up with this hardship as best I can." That's reasonable, isn't it? I'm not saying that you have to undergo an extreme Milarepa trip, but somehow you should face difficulties with the attitude, "As long as it's beneficial for others, I'll put up with it; it doesn't matter. After all, that's the reason

I became a monk, a nun. I've given up serving just one person; one woman, one man. What I really want to do is to serve for the benefit of the majority, for all sentient beings, as much as I possibly can." That is truly the right attitude.

I am not criticizing you. When people gather from all over the world, the dualistic mind is naturally there. Some eat tsampa; some eat pizza; others like hamburgers. There are many cultural distinctions. It is difficult; I'm not blaming you for anything. It's understandable that being in a group such as this can create difficulties; we can't make our differences into some kind of multicultural soup. But although these differences exist, we're trying not to emphasize culture here. Instead, we're trying to focus on the essential aspects of Buddhadharma. That is the most important thing; that is why we've gathered here for this Dharma Celebration. Lord Buddha's Dharma wisdom is the only reason we've come together. Why else would you bother with a Third World Tibetan monk? No; you have Dharma in your hearts, so we've all come here to live together in the spirit of the lam-rim, understanding that all mother sentient beings are equal in desiring happiness and not wanting misery. To the extent that we all share this attitude, we're very fortunate.

THE RESPONSIBILITIES OF THE SANGHA COMMUNITY LEADERS

The abbot and the gekyö should also have compassion for the Sangha community, thinking, "What is the best way for me to help them with their education, make them happy and, at the same time, make them comfortable?" Being an abbot or a gekyö is an incredibly big responsibility, and to do this job you have to understand how to take care of monks and nuns both physically and mentally. If you're concerned with only their mental well being, there will be difficulties; if you think they should be leading an ascetic, Milarepa-like existence, it will be extremely difficult. We're not living in Tibet. In French society there is no room for Milarepas. If you try to live like Milarepa in France, they'll arrest you. You just can't do a Milarepa trip in the developed world.

You can see, it's not easy to take care of the Sangha community. The Sangha community doesn't involve only yourself; it involves everybody, hundreds of people. The abbot, the gekyö and the monastery management should know how to care for both the physical and the mental requirements of monks and nuns. It is important to be concerned with both and not to become a Dharma fanatic.

The abbot, the organizers and, in fact, every Sangha member who has some ability and talent should have the attitude, "Besides pursuing my own education, it is important that I serve the Sangha, especially future generations. I can see through my own experience how beneficial it is to be a monk or nun, so I want to serve the Sangha by ensuring that those who come after me have perfect monastic facilities for study and practice."

The Catholic Church provides an excellent example of how to take care of monks and nuns. They put incredible emphasis on this and have a lot of valuable experience. Don't look at Catholics as bad examples; that's a mistake. We should take advantage of the good aspects of Catholic monasticism by integrating them into our Dharma communities.

The Sangha community leader needs to be flexible. If some Sangha members prefer to do certain kinds of work, provided they are qualified, you should let them do it, rather than forcing them to clean or do something else. Take people's wishes and abilities into consideration. As time passes, people's attitudes and behavior change, so as people develop, you can change their jobs accordingly. In some ways the Sangha is like a baby. Babies grow; babies change; their minds and abilities develop. The leader should also remember this when assigning tasks in the monastery.

However, monks and nuns themselves have the right to determine the best schedule for themselves; they have the right to say whatever they want, as long as it benefits the majority. It is wrong for the abbot or gekyö to force some nonsensical schedule onto the community. All of us have to take responsibility. Especially you people; you are no longer young, so try not to act like children. You should both dedicate yourselves to and act for the benefit of the majority. I feel that you have incredible potential and are largely responsible for establishing Dharma in the West for the benefit of future generations. I have great expectations of you, but my expectations are realistic and not at all exaggerated.

There are different ways of practicing and growing in the Dharma. Some people can meditate; others are better at organizing. Both can become Dharma. Mahayana means the great view, the universal view. There is an enormous amount of space in the Mahayana to accommodate different forms of practice, almost enough room for each person to have his or her own unique individual path. Such was Lord Buddha's incredible skill. So don't think that monastery rules are oppressive and that they prevent you from expressing your own intuition. That is wrong. We should—in fact, we do—allow you to express yourself. Don't think of the monastery as a concentration camp. On the contrary, monastic life is blissful, I tell you. It's true. We say that people who live in monasteries are completely protected; monastic life allows you to progress in the right direction without interference. That's what a monastery is really all about. For people whose lives are a disaster, though, monastic life is like a thorn in their side, like being in a concentration camp.

Certain aspects of monastic life can be changed. You yourself can change things for the better and, since we exist in order to benefit others, even the general public can make suggestions, as long as they are offered with great compassion and an eye to the future.

EDUCATION

What about the monastery's education program? I think balancing the three wisdoms of hearing, analytical contemplation and meditation is the most important thing. In the monastery, these three must be balanced. Simultaneously, they must also be exercised. You shouldn't have the attitude, "First I'll study for ten or twenty years; then for the next thirty years I'll analyze what I've learned; finally I'll meditate until I'm a hundred." That's a common misunderstanding.

It's true that the Sakya Pandita said, "He who meditates without first studying is like an armless rock climber," but many people, even learned geshes, misinterpret that statement. They'll tell you that the first thing you have to do is to learn stuff; that it's almost criminal to meditate without first studying. Of course, it's true that you can't make Coca-Cola without first having heard about Coca-Cola, that you can't meditate without having listened to Dharma teachings. But it's a misinterpretation to conclude from this that you have to study for twenty years before you can do any analytical contemplation and then only after another twenty years of that, say when you're sixty, can you begin to meditate. That is completely wrong.

Some Tibetans have this attitude, but not Lama Tsong Khapa. Even as a boy he meditated. He went into retreat on Manjushri and when he was sixteen, he met him: Manjushri appeared out of a rock in his cave. Remember that story? We term that a *rang-jung* [self-originated] Manjushri. Lama Tsong Khapa combined everything into his everyday life: listening, analytical checking and meditation. He put all three together. We should do the same: every day, all three should be practiced. Don't go a long time doing one without the others. That's a wrong conception.

Even when I was a boy at Sera Monastery, I was a victim of these misconceptions. I used to love praying, but I had to keep my small prayer book hidden from my uncle who took care of me because he didn't like me sitting in meditation position, doing my prayers. He'd tell me I was crazy; that—there's a Tibetan expression for this—"When your hair goes gray, that's when you meditate." How stupid! So whenever he came in, I'd hide my prayer book under the long philosophy pecha that I was supposed to be studying. I was OK as long as he didn't know what I was doing! That was a complete misconception.

For me, it is difficult to study philosophy and do nothing else. Sometimes in debate, while someone was making an argument, I'd completely space out, not knowing how to debate against him. For two or three hours I would just sit there doing nothing. Combining prayer with study kept me down to earth, balanced, and I want you people to be the same. You have an excellent understanding of the three principal aspects of the path to enlightenment because of your

extensive lam-rim studies. If, on the basis of this fundamental understanding, you do some practice and a little philosophical study as well
every day, the lam-rim will become so beautiful for you.

In our own organization you can see that some people have an
incredible level of intellectual understanding, but their hearts are not
so much into the Dharma. Please, I have sympathy for you. I've been
watching all my students to see how they do. For example, some
people are like, "Oh, I want to learn Tibetan language, study all the
different subjects and then I want to practice everything." So I watch.
After a couple of years of study, they become expert in Tibetan
language, but they give up the Dharma. They never practice lam-rim;
for them lam-rim is nothing. I have seen this; it's amazing. Sometimes
the Dharma of people who study Tibetan language becomes Tibetan-
style—they never practice any more. I'm not criticizing everybody,
but there are definitely some people like that. It disappoints me. I
guess when they learned the Tibetan language they came to know all
about Tibetan samsara. Then, instead of becoming liberated, they got
caught up in Tibetan samsara.

You know, the history of every samsaric culture is not so good.
When you're caught up in a samsaric culture, you can't differentiate
between that culture's garbage thought and Dharma; you can't
distinguish one from the other. Sometimes people who have not
studied Tibetan but whose hearts are truly in the Dharma can better
integrate their lives with life in the West than can those who have
studied Tibetan language. Of course, I can't say it's always like this,
but I am saying there are different ways of looking at it.

Therefore, the organizers who structure life at Nalanda Monastery
should try to balance teaching, study, meditation and daily life. I'm

not going to go into the details of my own experience because the situation at Sera is different from that in the West, in France. We will need a different schedule, one that accords with our environment. We cannot make it Tibetan style. However, the Tibetan way is to have certain periods of intensive study and certain homework-like periods. For example, one month could be devoted to community study according to the monastery's schedule, the next to personal study in your own room. Then this cycle can be repeated. In that way, the intensity of the study cycle varies. Think about it; I'm not going into the details of it now. Perhaps I can another time, but not today.

Because the education program in our monastery is balanced, the Sangha we produce will be intellectually clean clear and, therefore, universally accepted. Because the Sangha practice on the basis of the pure thought that always puts the benefit of the majority first, their minds will develop and people will see that they are compassionate and dedicated. Those are the kinds of monks and nuns we want our monasteries to produce.

The syllabus should include both sutra and tantra; we have to take this opportunity to study tantra. Our monks and nuns should be perfectly educated in both sutra and tantra. That's the way to grow quickly in order to benefit others.

When you need to take a break from your studies for vacation, for FPMT organizational work or your own personal work, you should not leave the monastery without the permission of the abbot or the gekyö. They should investigate the situation and decide with compassion what is of most benefit for you.

DEVELOPING THE SANGHA ORGANIZATION

It is very important that everybody contribute something to the development of our organization. For example, some monks and nuns have their own money and can take care of their own food, clothing and so forth. Others do not. Both those who have their own money and those who don't should work for, say, two or three hours a day for the benefit of the organization, with the aim of creating a strong Sangha community. If you are really dedicated, you can always fit everything in. But we are lazy; therefore, we rationalize. We can't even manage to do a one-hour puja. Don't you think you're rationalizing when your mind finds it too difficult to spend an hour at the Sangha community puja? Can you imagine! "I don't have time; an hour is too long." You're going to say that, aren't you? That's completely unrealistic; no compassion.

Most Western monks and nuns who come to India and Nepal tell me that they shouldn't have to work for their food and clothing because in Tibetan monasteries the monks don't have to work. "The monks in the Tibetan monastery in Boudha don't have jobs; why should we?" My goodness! What can I say? Can you live on black tea and tsampa? Can you? You'll be dead the next day. Tibetans can live like that. Look at Tibetan monks' faces: you can see that they eat only tsampa and black tea! You Injis can't do that. Your pink skins come from good, nutritious food! You couldn't survive on a Tibetan monastic diet.

I think you are capable of doing what needs to be done because your society has given you a good education; don't waste your time and energy trying to be Tibetan. It's unrealistic. It costs $500 a month for you to eat the way you've been brought up—not here in India, but in the West it does. Who's going to give you that money? Think about it scientifically. It's not part of Western culture for parents to work in order to support their adult children. And anyway, you're capable of supporting yourselves. If you really can't work because you're crippled or you've broken your leg, perhaps that's an exception. But you are so well educated; it's not good if you don't take care of yourselves. Of course, if you are from a rich family, you can ask them to support you. But if your parents are not well off, it is not their responsibility to take care of you. This just does not happen in Western culture.

Whether you have money or not, in the monastery you should give up your selfish needs and work to help others as much as you can. This is so important. Unless you can't see the benefit of having a community of monks or nuns. Is a Sangha community important or not? Can you see that or not? I'd like to know what you think. Yes, it is! It is so worthwhile. But this is not Lama Yeshe's effort. You people think that only Lama Yeshe can do it. I can't do anything. All I do is talk, "Blah, blah, blah...." It's you who have to act to make the community successful; it is in your hands. I can't do it; it's your responsibility. But it is really worth doing.

You should not think of just yourselves. Let's say I think only of myself. Why would I bother with you people, running after you all the time? I could disappear into a cave, go to the beach, sleep, be comfortable. That would be better than this. However, I feel it is necessary, somehow, that you should act to benefit others as much as you can and not always be obsessed by the pursuit of your own pleasure, always "Me, me, me." That's wrong, that's wrong. Try to benefit others as much as you possibly can; that is the most important thing. You have a choice: help yourself alone or benefit many people. Choose to benefit the many.

Remember what it says in the *Guru Puja*? "If it benefits even one sentient being, I will spend eons in hell." Remember that verse? It is so powerful. The way the Panchen Lama put that text together is incredible. "To bring Dharma to the West, for the benefit of the entire world, I am prepared to give up my own comfort." Think like that. You are more important than I am in bringing Dharma to the West. This is true. You people can live more realistically in your own culture than I can and you relate to other Westerners better than I do. Anyway, I'm about to die, so I can't do it. It's best if you feel, "I myself am responsible for bringing the Dharma to the West. That's the reason I became a monk; that's the reason I became a nun." It has great significance if you dedicate yourselves in that way. If you develop that sort of motivation, the appropriate actions will follow spontaneously; you won't have to force yourself.

Don't think that it is a bad thing for monks and nuns to work for their bread and butter. Who else is going to take care of you? Should mother sentient beings serve you? In the West there is no such thing as someone being someone else's servant.

Look, I am convinced that we can completely bring Dharma to the West; you people have convinced me. You are the nuclear energy of this movement. When you got ordained, you decided to dedicate your entire lives to the benefit of others. Remember? We taught you to have that attitude and you said the words when you got ordained, didn't you? You said, "For the benefit of all mother sentient beings I am becoming a monk/nun." Did you say that or didn't you? OK, you said it—we can agree on that!

You don't have husbands or wives; your lives are not committed to just one person. Don't think that you're married to me! You're free of me, aren't you? You understand what I mean. It's true. That's the point: you are completely free. What you have to do is dedicate yourself, without discrimination, to all mother sentient beings; that is your job. I truly feel that to bring Dharma into the Western world, you have to be living in some kind of purity. That purity gives power to your words and then you can offer Dharma to the West.

A LIVING DHARMA FOR THE WEST

Intellectual Dharma has already reached the West. In many cases, Western professors know the subject better than you do. But words are not Dharma; we need something behind the words. We need the kind of energy force that can be developed organically only through living purely in the Dharma. That is truly the root of the Dharma and its spread to the West. I have great expectations that you are the people to do it; please, think about it.

The Dharma we are trying to bring to the West is not simply intellectual Dharma. Intellectual Dharma is already there, in universities all over the world. I want you to understand. What we need is for the living experience of Dharma to touch the human heart organically and to eradicate people's dissatisfaction. This is the Western world's great need. Without your living in the Dharma, without your having a certain degree of experience, you cannot give Dharma to others. It is not possible. That is why, when you live in the Sangha community, the abbot or gekyö should be involved in deciding who goes where to teach. If you just do your own trip, you're in danger of turning Dharma into Coca-Cola.

Of course, you need to be well educated so that when you go to different places to teach you will have at least an intellectually clean-clear comprehension of the subjects you are talking about. Otherwise, you might start spreading misconceptions and then, instead of benefiting the Dharma, you will damage it.

We are a serious phenomenon. Don't think you're playing games with Tibetan monks, with Tibetan Mahayana Buddhism. This is not a joke. We should dedicate as much as we possibly can, in whatever way—words, deeds, intellect, meditation—for the sake of sentient beings; we should utilize our lives for their benefit. If you do whatever you do with sincerity, that is good enough. Without sincerity, many things become not good enough. There's no dedication.

This program, the Enlightened Experience Celebration, was created principally to benefit monks and nuns. I thought it extremely important that my monks and nuns receive a truly complete education. Then I won't be worried; wherever you go, you will take the light of Dharma with you. That is the main point. And in addition, we organized this event so that lay students could also attend.

Let's stop here and continue tomorrow.

THE ADVANTAGES OF MONASTIC LIFE: PART TWO

THE PURPOSE OF NALANDA MONASTERY

It is important that we consider how to present Dharma in the West. You can't just say, "Oh, this director invited me to come and give teachings. OK, I'll just go." This has happened many times, but I'm not sure that it's appropriate. Therefore, I wanted to say a little about education at Nalanda Monastery.

What is the purpose of Nalanda Monastery? It is a center for education, for Buddhist studies. Ideally, this means that eventually all the Sangha will become teachers. Come on! I want you to understand this. Now, being a teacher doesn't mean only being an intellectual words teacher. There are many different ways in which you can teach. Generally, however, I expect everybody to be well educated. There is a great demand for teachers in our centers; we are very short of them. Are you aware of this or not? Everybody should know this. Then you will put more energy into trying to benefit others instead of being lazy. The world's need for Dharma teachers is great.

The way this should work is that centers that need teachers should send their requests to the monastery and the abbot and gekyö should decide who goes out to teach. That's a good idea; it prevents people from doing their own individual trips. Of course, the center director can specify the qualifications or even the person required—"He or she is best for us because of the way we communicate"—something like that. For people to do their own trip is not so good. Also, this is not some kind of competition; we are just trying to be as beneficial as possible.

I feel sometimes that Western teachers are more suitable for Western beginners. They are oriented to the culture and may be more acceptable to new students: "This is just what I need; I can use this." We should encourage Westerners to do this kind of thing. Of course, Tibetan lamas can still come to give advanced teachings, but there are limitations to this as well. Therefore, we should hurry to educate ourselves well so that we can be of maximum benefit to others.

In our Sangha community, many students are already experienced in giving lam-rim courses. They have been teaching and I'm very happy about that. They are growing. Some Sangha members have intuitively understood that they should teach; I didn't have to push them. But others don't understand that they should teach and worry about it: "Lama said everybody has to teach. How can I possibly become a teacher?" Don't worry. Whatever your ability, just do as much as you can with your life. To my way of thinking, that's good enough. You don't necessarily have to push yourself to accumulate intellectual knowledge. We have room for people to serve the Buddhadharma in many different ways.

In the future, if we organize the monastery situation well, benefiting others through your education will also provide your bread and butter. Do not feel that, just because you cannot take care of yourself at the moment, your life as a Tibetan Buddhist monk or nun will always be economically difficult. That kind of mind arises sometimes; it's not so good. It's quite right to think about the situation, but many people in the world need teachers and, if you are well educated, they will support you. If a center applies for a Sangha member to come and teach, the center should take care of that person's airfare, food, clothing and stipend. Sangha should have a big view. If you educate yourself well and serve others, they will take care of you; it's natural. You offer something, you benefit others—others will benefit you. That's the cyclic nature of samsara.

You people have to figure out for yourselves a constructive approach to all this. I am concerned for your welfare, but since I'm too ignorant to take care of even myself, how can I possibly know what's best for your future?

Of course, we can quote Shakyamuni Buddha, where in one sutra he guaranteed that even if the amount of arable land on earth is reduced to the size of a fingernail, as long as his Sangha practice purely, they will never go hungry. Is that true or not? Come on! It can't be true! Well, I don't know if Lord Buddha was correct there or not. I have some doubt as to whether those words were true or not, because in my observation, many Sangha who have been practicing and studying sincerely have encountered trouble in getting the means of living, such as food, clothing and benefactors. Are there some who have experienced this kind of trouble? Well, in Western culture there's no custom of sponsoring monks and nuns; it's difficult. These days, even in Tibetan culture it's difficult. It used to be that Tibetan monks and nuns had it pretty easy, but not any longer.

I don't think we should go bananas worrying over whether or not someone will take care of us. These days all my Sangha are intelligent, they know what's going on in the world; they are educated to a certain extent...at least to primary school level! So who worries? You people are capable of taking care of yourselves. We don't need two or three of everything, but we do need to take care of our bodies and not get sick. You should take care of your body. You don't need to think you're a great meditator and try to lead an ascetic life, and thereby damage your nervous system. On the one hand, you talk about your precious human rebirth; on the other, you destroy your body. That's stupid.

I AM THE SERVANT OF OTHERS

Monks and nuns should be practical in taking care of themselves, socially acceptable and work for the benefit of the majority. If the Sangha cannot work for the benefit of others, then what's it all about? Honestly, you have to have the motivation, "I am the servant of others." Perhaps, instead of OM MANI PADME HUM, that should be our mantra. We should repeat over and over, "I am the servant of others, I am the servant of others...." I think I'm going to make this the monks' and nuns' mantra, make them repeat it a million times; make them do the retreat of this mantra, "I am the servant of others."

Sometimes monks and nuns have wrong conceptions. They consider that to be holy you have to live alone, leading an ascetic life. That's not necessarily so; we don't need to do that. Some people have this fantasy that by becoming a Tibetan monk or nun they have become some kind of great yogi. What makes a great yogi is dedication to others. Without dedication to others, there's no way for you to become a great yogi or yogini. It's impossible.

Maybe you think that serving others is impractical, that it doesn't work. It works; it works. There is less pain in your mind. If somebody asks you for a cup of tea, for some help, instead of pain, anger and irritation, you feel bliss. If you get annoyed when someone asks for help, it shows you have no dedication.

You should be practical. Sometimes lay people criticize monks and nuns because they think they're hopeless—they come home, eat and drink, but don't do anything to help. They don't even wash their own dishes; they leave them for others. They space out, say a few words about Dharma, blah, blah. Lay people don't understand. That is Western culture.

I tell you, there is a big difference between the way Westerners look at Dharma and the way Eastern people do. Your parents don't accept what you're doing because they think you're hopeless, stupid, not taking care of your life. That's what they worry about. Your parents love you. They want you to be practical, to take care of yourself. Have you heard lay people criticize the Sangha? I have. They're right, up to a point. Don't think that we're always right and lay people are always wrong.

Buddhadharma is practical, organic; it is something we can put into effect, here and now. Sometimes people have the misconception, "Ah, enlightenment is my goal," and look up into the sky, hands folded at their heart. "Up there is my husband, that is my Buddha, that is my Dharma, that is my Sangha. I don't care about anything down here." I call that fanaticism; their feet aren't on the ground. Be practical, OK? Fanaticism is ego, so arrogant, unreasonable, intangible; such people are simply dreaming. Perhaps it's because in Tibetan Buddhism we say, For the sake of all mother sentient beings I should quickly become Buddha, therefore I'm going to practice...some sadhana or other. Maybe this sadhana way of thinking is a Western misunderstanding. I don't know. Perhaps Mahayana Buddhism produces spaced out sentient beings instead of constructive organic flowers...or am I being too extreme?

We should be aware of what lay people think. But I do understand that it can sometimes be a little paralyzing for a monk or nun to live in a community where the majority are lay people. You are the only one; you feel insignificant. You try to fulfill your Sangha obligations, but you are nobody. You try to compromise with the lay community, but that doesn't work either. I do understand. I don't want my Sangha to be put into that kind of situation, but environmental and economic realities sometimes force you into it. With Nalanda, we finally have an opportunity to live away from such situations, so now, at least, you won't be able to blame the conditions for your difficulties. A monastic environment is extremely important.

Sometimes I get the impression that some of my Sangha think they won't be able to keep their vows if they get a job; that if they work, they will become disasters as monks or nuns. That is a completely wrong attitude; it shows they are suffocated by ignorance. Not only are we human beings, but Lord Buddha has also given us method and wisdom. We should somehow be able to figure out how to put work and keeping our ordination together, so that we avoid that suffocating alternative. Many students have given me this impression. I don't know if it's a true picture or not.

Monasteries exist in the West. How do they do it? Those monks and nuns are human; they eat, they sleep, they work. That is a true picture. So why don't we follow their example. Perhaps those Christian monks and nuns who work and still manage to keep their ordinations are more capable than we Buddhists. We should be ashamed of ourselves! Why don't you all become Catholic monks and nuns? Then you'd have no problems. I'm joking!

Anyway, what I am saying is that I want you to use your wisdom. I cannot tell you what to do. I do trust you to use your method and wisdom to come up with some way of establishing a Western monastery where we can both take care of ourselves materially and do our duty according to the vinaya. Can you motivate yourselves to accomplish this? I want you to generate a strong motivation, otherwise, we won't make it. There are too many obstacles, too many hurdles. I expect mistakes to be made. Even in bringing Dharma to Tibet, many bodhisattvas were killed protecting their ordination. Do you know the history of Buddhism coming to Tibet? They were actually killed because they would not break their vows.

If you compare your situation to that when Dharma came to Tibet, you will see how lucky you are. You have much better facilities and education and far easier lives than they did back then. You people are incredibly lucky. But I still want each one of you to be very strongly motivated at a personal level: "I myself (not we, but I) am responsible for bringing Dharma to the West. I've understood that Lord Buddha's wisdom is so powerful, it has brought me great satisfaction, and this is what the world needs more than anything else."

That doesn't mean that you change completely overnight and tomorrow walk around like some crazy evangelist. Just be relaxed, but at the same time dedicated. Then you'll be happy, no matter what sort of difficult situation you find yourself in—happy because you're serving others. If you do not have dedication, every situation is painful for you because the fundamental human problem is the self-cherishing thought, not wanting to share anything with others, which is the very opposite of dedication. The dedicated attitude makes everybody brothers and sisters. Without it, others become thorns in your flesh; they hurt you, they hassle you, especially if you are living together with many other people. You feel others are a hassle, the place is so crowded, it's like a concentration camp, Lama Yeshe is like a dictator, he comes around in the mornings saying do this and do that.... I am sure some of you might have had thoughts like this.

If you have a dedicated attitude, even should people accuse you of something or give you a hard time, it actually helps; it truly helps you. Personally, I really believe that we humans need to go through some hardships in order to develop understanding. If you're always going around spaced out and everything's too easy, you'll never learn. I learned only because Mao Tse Tung put me into such a learning situation. Otherwise, I was pretty easy-going. As long as my parents and uncle were giving me everything, I never learned a thing. Later, I checked back to see if I'd learned any Dharma at that time. I hadn't; I was just full of intellectual word games. Mao made me face real life. That time I learned a lot.

GRATITUDE FOR SANGHA

That's why I want you to be dedicated, but at the same time, happy. I don't understand why you're not happy. Being with each other, Sangha together, is such a warm, close feeling. I'm not a highly educated man, I'm not a highly realized person, but I feel so grateful just for the existence of other Sangha. We give each other strength. You have to understand, just by existing, you're helping each other.

It seems that some of you don't understand this. In other words, perhaps you don't understand the value of Buddhadharma. Those who don't feel that the Sangha community is so wonderful and that its members help each other don't understand Buddhadharma; they don't understand what is Dharma and what is not Dharma. Especially at times like this, when many monks and nuns have gathered together, you should recognize and respect them as actual Sangha. Perhaps you can't respect each individual, "He is Sangha; she is Sangha," and take refuge, but according to the vinaya you absolutely must respect the Sangha community as the Sangha object of refuge. When you received vinaya teachings from Tara Tulku in Bodhgaya recently, I'm sure he told you that four monks or nuns together are Sangha, didn't he? Well, don't just leave it at that. Inside your heart you should have the recognition, "That is the Sangha." Then you will feel respect.

I feel that you are very fortunate just to have met other people who are at least trying to live in the thirty-six precepts of novice ordination. It's unbelievable. In the world today, it's so rare. Do you think those brothers and sisters trying to keep the thirty-six vows are rare or not? Yes, they're rare. And if you understand the spiritual significance of this, you'll understand how valuable they are. I want you to understand: you are my brothers, you are my sisters, you are my husband, you are my wife, you are my dollars, you are my precious possessions, you are my everything! Everybody understands the value of those things, don't they? Well, each one of you is more valuable than all of those, more rare and precious than a million dollars. I feel I am so rich! It's true; I'm not joking. I really believe this. You people should feel extremely fortunate just being in this kind of situation.

Look around—where on earth can you find such a situation? These days the world is becoming incredibly impure, full of garbage thoughts, superstition and mutual hatred, so at least you people should try to feel compassion and loving kindness for one another instead of seeing each other as heavy burdens. You are the most fortunate people in the world.

Look at your present situation. In the morning you go to puja and they serve you tea there. As soon as that's over, your breakfast is ready. Then you go to teachings. After that, more tea is waiting. All you have to do is practice and take care of your mind; everything is there. Incredibly fortunate. Unbelievably fortunate. So, take advantage.

If you have a negative attitude toward a group of Sangha, that's the worst bad karma you can create, I tell you. According to what I was taught, if you think, "I hate those international Sangha," you are creating very heavy karma. From the Buddhist point of view, criticizing the Sangha is the most negative thing you can do. How do you know, amongst a group of Sangha, who is not a bodhisattva, who is not an arhat? I can't tell. Complaining, "These Western Sangha, they're no good, they're this, they're that..." is one of the worst things in the world you can do. You can point at individuals and say, "Lama Yeshe's no good," but when a group of seventy or eighty monks and nuns come together, how can you say they're no good? That's the heaviest karma you can create.

Honestly, I tell you, how many people in the whole world are keeping these thirty-six vows? How many are even trying? It is very, very rare. Normally we say that monasteries are so good. Monasteries are empty buildings. "Monasteries are good; monastery life is good."

An empty building is not a monastery. A monastery is good because a group of people is putting incredible positive energy into living in organic purity. Without people, it's just concrete and wood. That's not a monastery. Monasteries produce so many learned scholars, so many saints, because the people who live there help each other. Wood doesn't produce scholars; water doesn't produce saints.

Therefore, we're establishing Nalanda Monastery to produce many saints and scholars. That's why I called it Nalanda. We can be just like the ancient Indian monastery Nalanda, which produced such great Indian pandits as Atisha, Naropa and Shantideva. I really feel that our own monastery can produce such saints and pandits. I think so. I don't worry that the intellectual clarity of Buddhadharma can't reach the Western world. Westerners can comprehend anything that Tibetans can.

MONASTIC ROBES

Let me say a few words about robes. For the past few years I've had the experience of traveling around the world, living with my Sangha and with students in the Dharma center communities. I feel great compassion for my monks and nuns. Why? I'll tell you the reason. My monks and nuns try to be good human beings and keep their precepts responsibly, but when they go outside the center, people spit at them: "Oh, look at that poor man, that poor woman." I've seen it with my own eyes; it's incredible. I feel so sad. There's nothing wrong with those Sangha; the people who spit, they're the poor ones.

Why should I put my students into that kind of situation, where in their own society they are viewed as disasters rather than with respect, where people regard them as garbage? Recognizing their own profound human quality, students get ordained, but when they wear their robes, people put them down. I'm not sure it's worth it.

My understanding is that the Dharma we are bringing into the Western world should be Western Dharma, Inji Dharma, not Tibetan Dharma. Historically, Dharma never went from one culture to another without changing its external form. Internally, of course, the Dharma never changes; the essence of the Buddhadharma remains pure. But you can't make Germans or Americans eat tsampa; their stomachs aren't made for it. They don't need these external things. From Western society's point of view, people wearing robes are considered bad human beings, an insult to the rest of society.

We should be practical. I am not against the wearing of robes. I wear them myself. I'd be sick if I were negative towards what I wear every day. Well, I'm not sick; I'm happy with my robes. But what I'm saying is that when you are in your own country, working with and relating to people in regular society, I think it's stubborn to insist on wearing robes when people are putting you down and calling you a bad human being. Then they criticize Buddhism: "Buddhism produces bad human beings." That's what they're going to say, isn't it? They'll say, "Buddhism creates hippies," because they think monks and nuns are not responsible citizens, are socially unacceptable. Then Lord Buddha gets a bad reputation; do you want to give Lord Buddha a bad reputation?

We're serious people; we're not joking. You people are not practicing Dharma for Lama Yeshe; that's not the case. The Dharma you are bringing to the West is much bigger than just one person. You have to understand this. Psychologically, of course, each human being likes his or her own thing. For example, I'm a Tibetan monk; I think the Tibetan way is the best in the world; I want you to become Tibetan style. Then, when you act and look Tibetan, I'm happy, because you're supporting me. That's the most stupid way of thinking imaginable; it has no basis in reality.

I should be happy for you to be pizza-loving Italians; I am happy; I should be happy. A pizza-eating Italian who likes Dharma, whose mind is subdued, is incredible. And it's a true picture of Italians. Who wants artificial Italians? Anyway, they'll never change!

When monks and nuns are in a monastery or a Dharma center, they wear their robes; fine. But when they go out, they put on exactly the same clothes that everybody else is wearing and don't look any different from lay people. That's dangerous; I'm not happy about this. You should somehow signify that you're a monk or nun so that people can recognize you as such and you yourself remember. That was Lord Buddha's intention in having the Sangha wear robes. The clothes you wear should signify that you're ordained, distinguish you from lay people, remind you of your obligations and allow others to recognize you as a monk or nun.

My conclusion is that you need to wear something so that both other people will recognize you as a follower of some kind of path and you yourself will feel different from the laity. That will make your behavior completely different. We are not free from the influence of vibrations, so you should wear something that vibrates to show that you're a monk or nun. That will protect you from garbage thoughts.

Therefore, I am saying that it is very, very important to change your outside appearance according to your own culture. Last year I surveyed what people at various different centers thought and most

Dharma students agreed that the Sangha needed to modify the traditional robes because some people in the West were upset by them. From my side I didn't feel the need for change; change requires thought. But the reality is that most Western Dharma students thought the Sangha should wear something different from traditional robes. So what can you say? You mean well; you want to give a good impression. But, in fact, you upset people, so what can you do? If you've had the experience of wearing robes in public in the West, you'll understand this well.

Otherwise, you'll be thinking, "What is Lama talking about? We're happy here. We're so beautiful wearing our robes, I want to wear these robes, I want to wear what my guru wears, I don't want to wear something samsaric." However, you are from an entirely different culture. When Buddhism went from India to Tibet, the monks' robes changed completely; there's nothing Indian left. The same thing happened when Buddhism went to China and Japan, Korea and Vietnam. Of course, there are some similarities, but basically they are different. Why are they different? You cannot say their Dharma is bad Dharma. You cannot say that Tibetan Dharma is better, that it is better to wear Tibetan robes. That would just be an ego trip. Because climates and cultures vary, people compromise and come up with something that suits their environment.

Let's agree that we need to consider making some changes in the robes and that slowly, slowly we'll check out how to do that. When you are here in Dharamsala, you can wear exactly the same robes as Tibetans wear; Tibetan people will be very happy. But you are not Tibetan; don't think you are Tibetan. You're going to spend most of your life in the West, in your own country. Therefore, think about it.

For example, the *shem-thab*. Thai monks don't wear those as do we Tibetans; they don't wear zens, either, so what's the big deal? The most important thing is that the robes you wear should signify, or identify, you as a monk or nun. Ultimately, of course, robes don't mean anything.

We should experiment. We should invite some lay people to give their opinions on whether the Sangha should wear this or that. It's good for the people to judge. If the majority doesn't like you wearing these robes, if it makes them angry, is that profitable or not? It's not so good if the way you dress upsets them.

Lay people are very important when it comes to interacting with our monks and nuns. You can't say that monks and nuns are everything and that lay people are nothing, so therefore we're just going to do our own trip. You'd be wrong there. We are not beyond society. We are in society; we are linked with lay people. Lay people should also accept us. They're not stupid. They're concerned about Buddhadharma; they want Buddhadharma so much.

There's a Tibetan admonition, "Do not do anything to destroy the laity's faith and devotion in the Dharma." Monks and nuns have to be aware of that and should not create the karma of destroying lay people's faith in the Dharma. Lord Buddha himself taught that the Sangha should be socially acceptable. Society should feel, "Monks and nuns are so good; they are our object of refuge." We should always remember that and act accordingly.

Let's do a few questions and answers. Sometimes I get a bit extreme and talk nonsense, which just makes you angry. Well, I don't want to do that, so please express anything that will be of benefit to all of us.

Q. I think hair length, especially for women, may be an even more important issue than the robes.

Lama. That's true. I think some Sangha in the West have already started keeping their hair a little longer. We should understand why they do this rather than criticize them; we have some experience. Many nuns are working in society, some as center directors, and they've had to grow their hair a little in order to relate better to people they encounter. I feel that's perfectly acceptable; don't you? Good. It is very important that we understand each other; then there won't be problems amongst us. That's the best way. We should understand what each different country considers good behavior for monks and nuns and act accordingly, in order to benefit society.

Q. Lama, I hope that you will organize a meeting with lay people to discuss the robes.

Lama. Good idea. Lay people love Dharma; therefore, they love Sangha. They want their Sangha to have the best behavior in the world. We should feel that Sangha and lay people make up one society. Within a society there can be all kinds of different groups, but we should still feel the unity of being one family.

Q. If new-style robes were adopted, would they be the same in all Western countries?

Lama. We'd have to make a decision on an international level. When people from many different countries have agreed, then we can change. You don't need to wear Tibetan-style robes. But of course, we can do this gradually; there's no need for any radical changes. For example, even when we've changed, if some people still want to wear

Tibetan robes in the monastery, OK, let them. But you have to think about what changes to make.

Q. Sometimes it's hard for a new monk to know how to behave.

Lama. Guidance has to come from the older monks, and even though we don't have any really old Western monks, our senior ones do have much more experience than those newly ordained. Historically, older monks have always taken responsibility to see that new ones are properly nurtured to facilitate their spiritual growth. I feel I should do more, but it's difficult for me to get around to all the places where there are Sangha. Therefore, older monks and nuns should take responsibility for the young ones. If you go to the monasteries in south India, you'll see the opposite to what you'd normally expect: that in making sure that they get educated and have the means of living, the older monks are almost servants to the young ones. So far we've not been able to do that, but we definitely should.

Q. How much contact should there be in the future between Western monks and nuns? Should we have different monasteries?

Lama. There should be separate monasteries. We already have some fifty monks and fifty nuns, so we should definitely have a broader vision. In the future we're going to have many more; both the monks' and the nuns' communities are going to grow...by thousands, millions! So we have to figure out how we're going to take care of them. If you check out why you got ordained, you can see that it's logical that others will also become monks and nuns. As our organization grows and facilitates the spread of Dharma, as we produce more and better-educated teachers, it's only natural that there'll be more monks and nuns.

Therefore, it's your responsibility to create conducive conditions for the future Sangha. You may have faced difficulties coming up during this early time, but we have to establish better facilities for those coming after you, separate places for monks and for nuns. Basically, the nuns are responsible for the future nuns and the monks for the future monks, but since we're a Sangha community, we have to help each other. Nalanda Monastery in France is only the beginning. Not everybody wants to go to France. For one thing, the language is too much!

So, in the future, we're going to have Nalanda Monasteries in each European country, in Australia, in all Western countries. It will happen through the power of Buddhadharma, not just because I wish it. I just let go. Don't think Lama Yeshe wants a million monks and nuns. Who'd want all that trouble! But think about why you became monks and nuns; it's interesting. Then you can see how in the future many others will want to do it. Therefore, we should dedicate ourselves to creating better facilities for them.

Getting back to the problem of older Western monks and nuns not taking care of the younger ones, I think this is partly a result of cultural influence. In Tibet, as I mentioned before, senior monks and nuns take great care of the young ones. When I saw that the older Western Sangha didn't do this, I went into culture shock; I didn't understand that. It's not that we don't have older monks and nuns— we do. But they have no ambition to look after the new ones. What do you think about that? Let's hear from one nun and one monk.

Q. Well, it's not only that the older nuns don't want to take care of the new ones; sometimes the young ones don't want to be told what to do.

Lama. Yes, that's possible. What about the monks?

Q. I've found that older monks have been helpful when I've asked.

Lama. Yes, that's right. Perhaps if new monks ask older ones respectfully, they respond. We should develop good relationships with each other like that.

Q. When I was the gekyö at Kopan, it was the older monks and nuns who created the most trouble, so from that point of view it was difficult to respect them.

Lama. Yes, that's a good example. Sometimes it's true that older monks and nuns don't cooperate for the benefit of the group—they make incredible rationalizations based on their own individual trips. I've seen it myself. But I hope that the situation is changing, that older monks are becoming more concerned for the benefit of the majority than for their own trips.

Q. Sometimes the older Sangha may not realize that they're the senior ones; they might still think they're fairly new. But when you look behind you, you can see that there are many young ones there.

Lama. That's true; that's a good example. That definitely happens. They still think they're young. Anyway, I just want to emphasize again that I want the senior monks and nuns to take responsibility for ensuring that the future generations of Sangha are comfortable and well educated for their own growth and for the benefit of others.

THE BENEFITS OF BEING ORDAINED

This essay was prepared by Rinpoche for publication in Mandala, September-October 1996. It was initially dictated to Ven. Roger Kunsang and then amplified with the help of Ven. Paul LeMay.

If you talk to Westerners about the life of the Buddha and the twelve deeds—the circumstances of his birth, his life as a child, his marriage and the birth of his child, then his renunciation of the householder's life, becoming a monk and so forth—they might think that ordination as a Buddhist monk or nun is only for Asians. Because Buddha lived in India, they might think that it's an aspect of Eastern culture unrelated to the West. Moreover, because Buddha lived 2,500 years ago, they might also think that ordination is no longer relevant today. This is common, a normal way to think for people who don't understand the mind or know about karma.

It's the same when we describe the hell realms. Because the Buddha explained them in ancient times, people now think that they're simply an outmoded concept. If the hells don't exist, it means that nobody is creating the karma to be reborn there. In other words, everybody must have developed stable realizations. Why does it mean that? Because in order never again to be reborn in the lower realms, you must have attained at least the third, or patience, level of the path of preparation. (There are five levels of the path to liberation; the path of preparation is the second of these. The path of preparation itself has four levels, of which patience is the third.)

Two thousand years ago, Jesus Christ also revealed living in ordination as a method of practice. As a result, many Christian monasteries and nunneries were established, and over the past two millennia this still viable tradition has produced many saints.

People who say that ordination is no longer relevant in the modern world misunderstand its purpose. This method was taught by both Buddha and Jesus to protect us from delusions, to prevent us from harming ourselves or others. As a result of the karma of not harming others, we receive the immediate benefit of not being harmed by them and experience great happiness and peace. Of course, there are long-term benefits as well: rebirth in the upper realms, liberation and enlightenment.

Nevertheless, some people will still ask why today, when lay people can study and practice Dharma and attain enlightenment, is it necessary to live an ordained life?

It's true that some lay people can practice well, but that doesn't mean all lay people can practice well. Most lay people find it difficult. But just because Buddha and Jesus revealed the method of ordination doesn't mean that everyone should become monks or nuns either. Everybody can't become Sangha because everybody doesn't have the karma to become Sangha. To do so you need a lot of merit and no inner obstacles. If there are no obstacles in your mind, there will be no outer obstacles to your ordination.

The main point here is that until you have developed a stable realization of the three principal aspects of the path in your mind, to practice Dharma properly you need to spend a lot of time away from the objects that induce your delusions to arise. This is especially true for beginners, but in fact applies to anybody not yet liberated from samsara. Hence, the need for monasteries and nunneries, caves and hermitages, and the discipline that goes along with living in such ascetic environments. And by living in such places, you can easily see the importance of morality.

To actualize the fundamental paths, you need a great deal of study and meditation. For that you need much time and conducive circumstances. The most important thing is for your mind not to be distracted. The more negative karma you create, the more barriers you erect to your own realizations. That makes it much longer and more difficult for you to experience even samsaric happiness, let alone the bliss of liberation from samsara.

Therefore, the more you live in pure ordination, the less negative karma you create. By renouncing life as a householder and living as Sangha, not only do you create less negative karma, but you also cut down a lot on external work and other activities. This leaves you much more time for meditation and study; you have fewer distractions. Thus, there are many advantages to being ordained: more time to study and meditate, more time to develop your mind.

One of the most important meditations that you need to accomplish in order to really develop the path to enlightenment in your mind is mental quiescence. To realize shamatha, you need much discipline, protection and morality; you have to eliminate many distractions. Even for an hour's good meditation you need to cut distractions, apply discipline and renounce attachment. If you follow attachment, you can't meditate for even a minute. If your mind is occupied by desire objects such as boyfriends or girlfriends, you can't meditate for even a second. So, on the basis of that simple example, you can understand how living in ordination as Sangha makes it much easier to practice.

For all this then, the environment becomes very important. To maintain the inspiration to remain Sangha, to continue practicing, to develop your mind in the path to liberation and enlightenment, month by month, year by year, to continue as a beginner whose mind is not stabilized in the three principal aspects of the path or calm abiding and so forth, you need the right situation. The environment has a strong effect on your mind. It controls the mind of the person who, let alone having no realizations, doesn't even practice the lam-rim.

Even if you have an excellent understanding of the lam-rim teachings themselves, if you don't practice, external objects will influence, control, overpower and overwhelm your mind. Whether you are a lay person or ordained, without choice you will seek out and run after objects of attachment. But as soon as you start to practice, to meditate on, the three principal paths—especially the basic one, renunciation—your mind becomes more powerful than external objects.

The moment you begin to apply the teachings of the Buddha in daily life, your mind starts to become more powerful than external objects and can overcome their attraction, no matter what those objects may be: living beings or non-living things, handsome people, beautiful flowers, whatever. Why? Because as long as you practice the lam-rim, your delusions remain under control.

As beginners, you need to both practice lam-rim strongly and keep away from disturbing objects. Your mind is weak because since beginningless time it has been habituated to attachment, not to the path to enlightenment. Therefore, your delusions are very strong, especially when you're surrounded by disturbing objects. Your intention or desire to seek liberation is very weak, but your wish for samsara, objects of delusion, pleasure and desire is very strong. Therefore, you need strong lam-rim meditation to subdue and control your mind and your attachment, and at the same time you need to retreat, to keep your distance from objects of attachment. If you don't withdraw from the internal suffering of attachment and desire, then living in ordination surrounded by objects of desire is like trying to get cool by sitting in front of a fire.

So of course, setting up a good external environment for Western Sangha is one thing, but individual Sangha members choosing to stay there is another. We can establish a perfect environment, but individual monks and nuns can decide not to stay there and stay instead in the wrong environment. Then, if your minds are weak, if you have no realizations or stability in the path, you will be overwhelmed by external objects. Delusions will take over your minds, you will follow the delusions and you will, therefore, be unable to practice Dharma or live in your vows.

Then, on the basis of this fundamental error, instead of enjoying your life and feeling how fortunate you are when you think of all the advantages that you will experience—the good results of liberation and enlightenment, the absolute certainty of a good rebirth no matter when you die—your life will become difficult and living in ordination will seem like living in prison.

Morality is a passport to success, a guarantee for an upper rebirth.

It's like a university degree that guarantees respect and a good job. The immediate, urgent thing is to stop rebirth in the lower realms: not only does morality guarantee you that, but it is also the basis, or foundation, for liberation and enlightenment. Therefore, it is extremely necessary to establish the right environment for practice.

The Buddha explained the many benefits of ordination in his sutra teachings and they are also enumerated in the lam-rim. In the twice-monthly so-jong ceremony, we recall the shortcoming of breaking our vows and receive inspiration by reciting these benefits. Such benefits include enjoying the glory of a radiant body, effortless fame, others' praise of our good qualities and the gaining of happiness.

If your moral conduct is pure, others will not harm you. This is an important point to note: to be harmed by others, you must have created the cause, that is, you must have harmed them. You should think of the logic of this. Just as a blind person cannot see, neither can an immoral person be liberated. Those who do not live in morality are like people without legs, who cannot walk wherever they wish. Just as a vase meant for holding jewels cannot hold anything if it is broken, similarly, since morality is the basis for all realizations, if you break your vows, you will be unable to achieve any Dharma realizations. Without the foundation of morality, there is no way to attain the sorrowless state of nirvana. These are but a few of the benefits taught by the Buddha and recited during so-jong.

It is the responsibility of each monk or nun to make a plan to protect him- or herself by living in the right environment. That is the purpose of monasteries and nunneries; that's why there are vinaya rules. They help protect your mind. By protecting, guarding, your mind, you free yourself from all problems, obstacles and suffering, ultimately liberating yourself from the oceans of suffering of each samsaric realm. You fulfill all your aspirations for happiness and bring much happiness to all sentient beings as well.

Many of the precepts in the vinaya that tell you what to do and what not to do were given by the Buddha in order to protect the minds of others. If you follow the vinaya rules, you prevent others from criticizing the Sangha, which, karmically speaking, is a very heavy object. Negative karma created with the Sangha as its object is extremely grave. If, however, the Sangha is careless with sentient beings' minds, feelings, happiness and suffering, it is easily possible to provoke their criticism. Therefore, since you, the Sangha, are responsible to guide the laity, you should follow the vinaya correctly. If you do, others will generate faith in their minds toward the Sangha, planting in their minds the seeds of liberation and enlightenment. It may even inspire them to follow the path by taking ordination themselves, since normally, sentient beings follow the Buddha's example of how to practice Dharma.

Being Sangha makes others respect you and, thereby, create much merit. The more purely you live in your ordination, the greater will be your power of success when you pray for others. Your prayers and pujas on behalf of others will be more likely to succeed. If you are living purely, you can achieve the result more easily; the mantras you recite will be more powerful. The deities, buddhas and Dharma protectors have to listen to your requests, have to help you. Because of your purity, they have no choice. Even if you don't make requests, they naturally have to serve and help you.

Also, since your life is pure, when sentient beings make offerings to you, they create even more merit, and also there is no danger to yourself in your accepting their offerings. If, as it says in the teachings, you do not live purely and then eat what is offered to you, it is like drinking lava or molten iron. It is said that you'd be better off consuming molten iron than consuming offerings made by others out of devotion.

Also, when you teach, you will have a much greater effect on people's minds than do lay people when they teach; there's a big difference. The people receiving the teaching see that the teacher him- or herself is living in renunciation. Lay people respect what you are doing, leading a life that they themselves cannot. Recognizing a quality that is hard to achieve, they will respect you for it. Also, lay students should learn to regard the Sangha in this way and allow devotion to arise. If lay people think that the Sangha do not have any special qualities and fail to make offerings to or support the Sangha, they miss out on a great chance to create good karma.

If lay people do not protect their own minds, do not practice morality themselves, even when they try to help others, they will be unable to offer them perfect service. When trying to help others, problems and difficulties will always arise because of ego and the three poisonous minds. Without Dharma practice, one can't really offer perfect service to others without running into problems. Whether one is the leader of a country or doing some other kind of public service, sooner or later problems will arise. Even in normal daily life it is like this: without morality, without protecting your mind, without some kind of discipline, you can't really find peace, satisfaction, happiness, or fulfillment in your heart.

If there were not a big advantage to being ordained, if it were not extremely important, why would Guru Shakyamuni Buddha have set that example? According to the Mahayana teachings, Buddha's showing that he reached enlightenment at Bodhgaya was not really when he became enlightened. In reality, he reached enlightenment an inconceivable number of eons ago. The reason he went through the twelve deeds—including renouncing the family life, shaving his head and becoming a monk—and taught the four noble truths was to teach us how to practice Dharma. And as I said before, it is not only Buddhism that teaches its followers to live as ordained persons in monasteries and nunneries.

Also, not only Buddhism teaches the attainment of the nine levels of meditative concentration and the development of shamatha. This practice is also common to Hinduism, where morality and discipline are also practiced along with renunciation, and can be accomplished without taking refuge in Buddha, Dharma and Sangha by simply developing detachment to pleasure, renunciation of the desire realms and thinking of the shortcomings of being in the form realm. Finally, by thinking of the shortcomings of remaining at any of the first three of the four levels of the formless realm, they attain what's called the "peak of samsara." But they cannot renounce samsara entirely; that's not taught in Hinduism. There's no mention of ultimate liberation, the five paths, or emptiness. And without an understanding of the Prasangika view, the highest of the four schools of Buddhist philosophy, there's no way to free yourself from samsara. Nevertheless, by studying the methods of other religions, without even taking into account the Buddhist way, you can see the great importance they too place on ordination, morality and discipline.

Therefore, generalizing that in the West, nobody should get ordained and everybody should practice as lay people is a wrong conception. This misunderstanding arises both from not really knowing what Dharma is, especially karma, and much more importantly, from lacking meditation experience or a realization of samsaric suffering, especially that of the lower realms, impermanence and death.

Even if a person has some understanding of Dharma but it is merely intellectual, then depending on the individual, the person's mind will remain the same, or get worse; the delusions can become even stronger than they were before. Thus, the person leads his or her life according to delusion: delusion becomes one's refuge, one's best friend, one's guru.

In this way, people's lives become very difficult and confused. Even if you are ordained, externally you might appear to be Sangha, with a shaved head, but inside you may be the opposite. Of course, nobody but yourself makes your life difficult; you imprison yourself in samsara through following delusion. Then, because of your experiences, which are actually the result of your not having practiced Dharma continuously, you start telling everybody else that it is not a good idea to be a monk, that it is better to practice Dharma as a layperson.

In Tibet we make tsa-tsas, clay images of buddhas and deities usually made from metal molds. From one mold we can make thousands of images. Making yourself a faulty mold by not practicing Dharma and then trying to cast others in your mistaken image is a bad way of making tsa-tsas.

Here's what makes it difficult to lead the life of a monk or nun. If you set your heart on attaining the bliss of nirvana, your life becomes easy; even if you run into problems, you can bear hardships with pleasure; they're not important to your mind. If, however, your goal is samsaric pleasure, then even if other people don't cause problems, you make your own life difficult. Even if others consider something to be OK, in your mind you see it as too hard. Therefore, how you find living in your ordination depends on the goal that's in your heart. If you change your goal from samsara to liberation or enlightenment and keep it there for twenty-four hours a day, you'll have no problem. If your heart is clear, your life will not be torn.

Naturally, you can't have both samsara and nirvana. As the Kadampa geshes liked to say, you can't sew with a two-pointed needle. You can't seek both the happiness of this life and the happiness of Dharma. If you try, what you lose is the happiness of Dharma.

Therefore, you cannot generalize and say that these days, especially in the West, ordination is irrelevant and everybody should practice as lay people. That is completely wrong.

A LIFE WELL LIVED

During the Most Secret Hayagriva retreat at Vajrapani Institute, September-October 1997, Lama Zopa Rinpoche offered the students the following advice. It came during Rinpoche's reading of a long commentary to the Most Secret Hayagriva sadhana, where it elaborates on the refuge section:

> Until we attain the state of the All-Pervading
>   Lord Samantabhadra,
> I and all sentient beings without exception equaling
>   the limitless sky
> Take refuge in the Three Jewels, the essence of rare sublimity,
> And in the entire assembly of mandala deities.

From beginningless samsara right up to this very second, my kind mother sentient beings and I have been under the control of the three poisonous minds. Motivated by the three poisonous minds, we have created various karmas. As a result, we have been taking various bodies from the peak of samsara down to the lowest realm, the vajra hell, and have been experiencing constantly the unbearable sufferings of samsara in general and those of the three lower realms in particular. Who has the power to save me and my kind suffering mother sentient beings from all this? Only the Guru Triple Gem, now abiding before me. Please, Guru Triple Gem, right now, protect me and my kind mother sentient beings from the extremely terrifying sufferings of samsara, particularly those of the three lower realms. From this moment on, until I see the face of Buddha Samantabhadra, I will never abandon my object of refuge, the precious and sublime Triple Gem, no matter what happens in my life—good or bad, happiness or suffering.

The Tibetan terms used here in the commentary, *zang-ngän*, can be interpreted in different ways. Generally, zang means good and ngän means bad, but they can also mean pure and impure, or happiness and suffering. Broadly, when related to our lives, good can mean having an easy life, where things go smoothly, and bad can mean a difficult life, where we encounter many obstacles and problems. However, what is good or what is bad depends upon the individual's interpretation.

From the Dharma point of view, if you spend your life creating more virtue than non-virtue, that's a good life. If last year you created more positive than negative karma, that was a good year; if yesterday you created more merit than negativity, that was a good day. Even if you spend only half your time in virtue, that's still pretty good. It just depends on how you look at it. If you compare yourself with someone who creates negative karma twenty-four hours a day, relatively, creating a few hours' virtue every day is a good life. A quarter of a day's virtue is obviously better than none at all.

So that's the general definition of the good life and the bad: the relative proportion of positive karma to negative. If, during a twenty-four-hour stretch, you are able to collect more virtue than non-virtue, then, even though you might feel exhausted, even though you might have almost died practicing Dharma, your life that day was good.

Look at Naropa, for example. He had to undergo twelve great and twelve lesser hardships in order to fulfill the instructions of his guru, Tilopa. Nevertheless, his was the best of all possible lives. Milarepa, too, had to face many difficulties. Under the orders of his guru Marpa, three times he had to construct and then immediately tear down that nine-story tower, all by himself. He was never allowed to come to teachings or initiations with the other students, was always beaten and scolded and never heard any praise, such as, "Oh, you are such a good disciple," or, "You have done excellent practice." Despite accomplishing whatever task he was set, all he ever saw was the wrathful aspect of his teacher. However, by following Marpa's advice to the letter and never allowing the slightest negative thought about him to arise, Milarepa attained enlightenment in that very lifetime. When you think about what constitutes a good life and what constitutes a bad, Milarepa's was the very best.

It's very important to know clearly the difference between a good life and a bad one. If your connotation is incorrect, if you have your own hallucinated opinion about it, you'll get very confused. You'll go in the wrong direction and as a result your mind will finish up empty of attainments, empty of realizations—completely empty of anything worthwhile.

Thus, you can interpret good and bad according to Dharma wisdom, the right understanding of the lam-rim and karma, or according to the view of attachment, ego and self-cherishing. Naturally, these two interpretations are completely opposite. Attachment's connotation of good and bad in particular is diametrically opposed to that of wisdom. This is where the confusion lies. If your faith in and understanding of Dharma are too weak, you'll find it easier to believe attachment's interpretation; if your faith and understanding are strong, you won't find it so difficult to follow wisdom's definition of good and bad.

Generally speaking, common people in the world at large follow attachment. To them, a good life is one where success is measured by external development—the accumulation of more, more, more: wealth, possessions, cars, friends, family, children, grandchildren, great-grandchildren and so forth—external, visible signs of prosperity. According to attachment, this is the best kind of life to lead. But what's behind this quest?

Actually, what everybody wants is peace, happiness and satisfaction in their hearts and minds. That's what everybody is looking for. The trouble is, most people don't know how to find it. The only method they have for finding fulfillment is external development. That's all they know because they lack a Dharma education. So, even though they want peace of mind and satisfaction, they have no method other than the external one. No matter what they do, they always finish up, as the Rolling Stones so aptly put it: "I can't get no satisfaction."

Say you spend years, perhaps your entire life, in retreat, or living in a monastery or nunnery—adhering to moral disciplines, keeping precepts, sacrificing a great deal of comfort and the pleasures of this life in order to lead a pure life. If you haven't renounced attachment, your mind will suffer a lot. From my point of view, that's still a good life. Because you have not freed your mind from the attachment clinging to this life, not separated it from worldly concerns, not made your mind healthy, you don't enjoy your practices or enjoy engaging in discipline. If, rather than associating with virtuous friends and good practitioners, you choose instead to stick to attachment and be friends with the eight worldly dharmas, then, even though physically your body may be in retreat or in a monastery, you won't experience peace or happiness in your heart.

As long as your mind is friendly with the attachment clinging to this life and the thought of the eight worldly dharmas, you will not be able to give up this life's pleasures and comfort in order to practice Dharma, follow morality and the advice of your virtuous friend, or offer service to the monastery or to the other monks and nuns. It is difficult for you to serve any sentient being when your mind is stuck in attachment instead of Dharma.

However, even though your mind makes it hard for you to enjoy your life or find happiness in your heart, if you still try to practice morality and follow monastic discipline, which supports and guides your mind and protects it from obstacles, it's still a good life. Similarly, when you have trouble staying in retreat, offering service to your virtuous friend, or working for sentient beings, if you persevere, you are again ensuring that your life will be good. Why? Because the merit you create will always bring good results.

If you are motivated more by attachment than by wisdom, you

may not find happiness or satisfaction in your heart and mind when you do your practices or keep your vows. Nevertheless, you are still leading a good life because what you are doing will bring the result of a good rebirth in your next life. Even if your mind is not completely pure, not completely renounced, not completely free of the thought of the eight worldly dharmas, the attachment clinging to this life, not completely ascetic, the result of your practice will definitely be good. Therefore, your life is a good one.

Of course, it takes time to develop a fully renounced mind. It takes strong, continual, intensive meditation, especially on impermanence and death as related to karma and the sufferings of samsara, particularly those of the lower realms, and on the preceding lam-rim meditations on the perfect human rebirth: the eight freedoms, the ten richnesses, the difficulty of receiving it, how it is highly useful and how it is difficult to find again. But the more strongly renounced your mind is, the further behind you leave the evil thought of the eight worldly dharmas, the attachment clinging to this life, the greater the peace, happiness and satisfaction you will find in your heart.

Similarly, the extent to which the eight worldly dharmas—praise and criticism, good reputation or bad, receiving material things or not, finding happiness and comfort or problems and discomfort—disturb you depends on to what extent your mind is following attachment. For example, the more you cling to being liked or well thought of, the more painful you will find being criticized; the stronger your wish to feel comfortable, the more you will hate discomfort. When things happen that attachment doesn't like—the opposites of the four desirable situations—the more disturbed you get, the greater the pain in your heart, the bigger your problems appear.

But even though you have not completely renounced the attachment clinging to this life, even though your heart is not completely detached from the evil thought of the eight worldly dharmas, even though you don't enjoy being in the monastery or nunnery or living in your ordination, as long as you try to maintain your practice, you are still living a good life; your efforts will yield the excellent fruit of a good rebirth in your next life. That's what I call a good life.

If you don't see it that way, you might decide to give it all up: "Oh, Dharma practice hasn't made me happy. After all these years of studying Tibetan Buddhism, taking teachings from the most qualified lamas, living in the monastery and keeping my ordination, I still haven't found satisfaction or happiness in my heart. Perhaps I should go to a mosque and try Islam." Then you abandon everything you've been doing and try living without rules or discipline, a completely free young guy or gal. You go from trying to free yourself from attachment to doing the opposite—living by delusion.

Of course, I'm generalizing. I'm not referring to everybody who has disrobed. Yet this is what commonly happens when people change their life. Still, it doesn't matter how excited you are, how much happiness you think you've found in external pleasures, you have to ask yourself: is this happiness from the Dharma point of view or from the point of view of attachment? You should analyze what you experience as happiness in this way.

So, even though you are excited to be free or to have physical comfort, great wealth and many friends, your life is motivated by an uncontrolled mind and you must consider the karmic result. If you don't analyze your life according to motivation and result but instead simply look at what's going on in your immediate surroundings, it may appear all right; it may look like you're enjoying yourself. But no matter how firmly you believe that you are happy and enjoying a good life, it's a complete hallucination. Even the happiness is a hallucination.

It is only if you don't think of your motivation or future karmic results that your life seems to be happy. A truly happy life is one that has a positive motivation and a positive result. From my point of view, from the Dharma point of view, that's a happy life. Naropa and Milarepa, who underwent such great hardships following their gurus' orders, had fantastic futures, the best futures. Theirs were the best of all possible lives, even though they had to bear so many difficulties.

Nevertheless, you can't purify your mind in just one day. You can't all of a sudden detach yourself from the attachment clinging to this life simply by living in a monastery or a nunnery or by becoming a monk or nun. It takes time. So until that happens, you too might have to bear many hardships. But if you don't meditate continuously and intensively on the graduated path of the practitioner of lower capacity, especially on impermanence and death and the perfect human rebirth, you will never be free from attachment.

In the meantime, you should enjoy living in morality, keeping your ordination, adhering to the monastic disciplines. All this protects your own mind and brings great benefit to others. Of course, the discipline you follow ought to be of benefit to your mind; it was created for that purpose. Thus, it is completely different from, for example, military discipline. The disciplines followed in the great monasteries of Sera, Ganden and Drepung and in the Upper and Lower Tantric Colleges were devised by incredibly learned holy beings in order to benefit the minds of those who adhered to those disciplines in order to develop their minds on the path to enlightenment. Other sentient beings benefit, too, because while you are practicing morality, you are abstaining from harming them. These are the aims of monastic discipline.

Therefore, while you are living under such conditions, even though part of your mind might be telling you that this style of life brings you no happiness or satisfaction, you should recollect the results that your practice will bring. Since you are abiding in the morality of not killing, not stealing and so forth, you know that there will be a good karmic result, that you will experience happiness in the future. Therefore, even though you don't feel happiness in your heart right now, you can be sure that you will in the future. That's the main point I am trying to emphasize.

These days, however, especially in the West, the only goal seems to be, "Does this make me happy right now?" That's the main goal: me, happy, now. It has to be right now, this very moment, today. Then on top of that comes the old-style psychology of cherishing yourself, pumping yourself up to feel important, the daily affirmation and so forth. However, the best way of taking care of yourself, the best way of loving yourself, is to practice Dharma.

When you practice Dharma, you are not rejecting yourself but rather looking after yourself in the best possible way. As you develop renunciation, you are liberating yourself from samsara. That's exactly what you need: without liberation, you will experience suffering continuously, again and again, without end. Meditating on emptiness is also the best way of taking care of yourself: developing the right view, you cut the root of samsara. What need, then, to mention generating bodhicitta, which leads you to the ultimate happiness of enlightenment? Beyond the three principal aspects of the path, what else do you need? What better than this is left for you to do? What higher goals can you achieve? What could possibly be better than liberation from samsara and enlightenment? What better way is there of taking care of yourself?

Whenever we practice Dharma in our daily lives, we're taking care of ourselves in the best possible way. As His Holiness the Dalai Lama often says, if you're going to be selfish, be smart about it. That means if you want to be happy, you should serve others, benefit others, and avoid giving them harm. That's the best way of ensuring your own happiness and of making your life successful. This is what His Holiness means when he talks about "wise selfishness."

What I'm saying is similar. Without the practice of Dharma, there is no happiness; without the practice of Dharma, you will never be happy. Therefore, the best way to find happiness, the best way to take care of yourself, the best way to look after yourself is to practice Dharma. Whenever you practice Dharma, you collect virtue; the infallible result of virtue is happiness—not only this life's happiness, but happiness in many lives to come. Karma is certain; good karma definitely brings happiness. Methods for happiness other than Dharma are unreliable.

Actually, other than Dharma, there are no methods for happiness. You can never achieve happiness from a method that is not Dharma. If it's not Dharma, it's non-virtue, and the only possible result of that is suffering. Therefore, whenever we practice Dharma in our daily lives, we are really taking care of ourselves in

A Life Well Lived

the best possible way, really loving ourselves. The only possible result of that is happiness.

Even if your attitude is simply that of seeking happiness for yourself—better future lives or your own liberation from samsara—you are still taking care of yourself and leading a good life. And if you are offering service to other sentient beings but finding no happiness in your life because your mind is impure, because you have not yet conquered ego and attachment, not yet renounced samsara, at least you are working for others. As long as you are working for the happiness of other sentient beings, you are still leading a good life.

Still, as above, you might feel, "I'm not enjoying this life; my heart isn't happy," or "My motivation is so impure," and as a result, stop working for others. If you then go and do something else, something which benefits neither yourself nor others, you will lose even the small benefit you were offering others through the efforts of your body, speech and mind, and your life becomes a complete waste of time.

Compare these two: totally wasting your life and doing something beneficial for others, even with impure motivation. If what you do becomes useful for others, you're still living a good life; others receive happiness from what you do. If you stop doing that and instead do something that has no benefit whatsoever, you completely waste the energy of your body, speech and mind. Everything you have spent on food, shelter, medicine and clothing from the time you were born up until the present is rendered completely useless; it didn't benefit you, it didn't benefit others.

Not only do you waste everything that you yourself have done,

93

but you also waste everything that your parents did. For all those years, from the time of your conception up to the present, they sacrificed their lives to look after you. They worked so hard, to the point of exhaustion, with great concern, fear and worry for your welfare. If you now spend your life doing something that brings no benefit to yourself or others, all your parents' efforts will be completely wasted.

Therefore, we should rejoice that we have met the precious Buddhadharma, especially the lam-rim, which integrates the entire collection of the 84,000 teachings of the Buddha into a coherent whole that allows us to practice without confusion and to attain the supreme goal of enlightenment. Through practicing the lam-rim, by purifying our negative karma and obscurations and accumulating merit through, for example, reciting the Vajrasattva mantra or the names of powerful deities, we can eradicate all our wrong conceptions, complete all the realizations of the path, especially bodhicitta, and work perfectly for all sentient beings. Every day, by listening to and reflecting and meditating on the lam-rim we benefit our lives enormously. By reading the lam-rim teachings for even a few minutes, a few seconds, we plant the seed of enlightenment in our minds. In those few moments of reading, we are also bringing great benefit to other sentient beings. And apart from meditating on the path, we can also offer service to sentient beings in many other ways. There is no question, therefore, that we should rejoice.

So, going back to the commentary, "...no matter what happens in my life, pure or impure" means that you must take refuge at all times. If you have broken your vows, or even if you are not a precept-holder but have created any of the ten non-virtuous actions or other negative karma, you still need to take refuge. In fact, at those times you should take refuge even more. You can't think, "I've created negative karma, I'm hopeless," and just give up, stop practicing Dharma. You still want happiness; you still don't want suffering. Therefore, at such times, you should take refuge more strongly than ever.

So whatever happens in your life, pure or evil, good or bad, happiness or suffering, take refuge—not just by mouth, not merely by words, but from the very bottom of your heart, beseech the Guru Triple Gem, "Please guide me, right now." Then, with this thought in mind, recite, "I and all sentient beings without exception equaling the limitless sky..." and so forth. This verse shows us how to take strong refuge. When you pray, the words that come out of your mouth and what you feel in your heart should be in harmony. What you say and what you feel should be identical; you must abide in the meaning of the words.

The main point of what I've been trying to say is that as long as you are living in your ordination or in a monastery or nunnery, even though you may not find happiness or satisfaction in your heart, your life is still worthwhile; it is still a good life, because the result of the good karma you are creating will be happiness in future lives. Not in just one life, but in many future lives. So even though you find life difficult and feel that you have sacrificed a lot of comfort and pleasure, your Dharma practice will definitely ensure a good future for you. In the long run, you will receive much happiness, good rebirths, liberation and enlightenment. Therefore, even if you find it difficult to practice and do not enjoy it, please do not become discouraged.

INTERNATIONAL MAHAYANA INSTITUTE

www.fpmt.org/IMI

The International Mahayana Institute (IMI) was founded by Lama Yeshe in 1973. The FPMT's first Western Sangha community was established at Kopan Monastery in 1974, where a group of about twenty monks and nuns from all over the world pioneered a program of study, meditation, and communal living. A small outpost was established in Dharamsala in 1976, and for the next few years IMI activity was based in India and Nepal.

In 1981, Nalanda Monastery was established in France, and in 1982, as a means of drawing his Sangha together, Lama Yeshe organized the first Enlightened Experience Celebration (EEC), which was attended by about one hundred Western monks and nuns. After the EEC, several monks returned to Nalanda, while a group of nuns established the Dorje Pamo Nunnery at nearby Vajra Yogini Institute.

Since then the number of non-Tibetan monks and nuns within the FPMT has gradually increased, and there are now several monastic communities:

- Nalanda (nalanda@compuserve.com)
- Chenrezig Nuns' Community (chenrezig@ozemail.com.au) and Thubten Shedrup Ling Monastery (tsl@impulse.net.au) in Australia
- Taipei Sangha Community (sanghaw@ms24.hinet.net) in Taiwan
- Thubten Shedrup Targye Ling (iltk@libero.it) at Istituto Lama Tzong Khapa in Italy
- Sera IMI House (Shedrup Zung Drel Ling, seraIMIhouse@yahoo.com) at Sera Monastery in India
- Kachoe Zung Juk Ling Abbey (anilaannmcneil@cs.com) in Canada.

The Lama Yeshe Sangha Fund helps support many Sangha members. The IMI also publishes a newsletter, *Sangha*, which helps its far-flung members stay in touch with each other.

Sangha and other IMI information is available on the FPMT web site, www.fpmt.org/IMI.

LAMA YESHE SANGHA FUND
Sangha supporting Sangha

"Only if the individual members of the Sangha community start looking after each other and take responsibility to provide for the community financially will substantial help come from the lay community."

—Geshe Lama Konchog

The Lama Yeshe Sangha Support Fund was established to enable members of the Sangha community to do retreat, study, or do work for the FPMT or IMI independent of their financial circumstances. How many people can be sponsored by the Fund depends entirely on how much money is available in the Fund. At this stage, there is not much, and most of it comes from benefactors in the lay community. It is vital that Sangha members themselves start contributing to the future financial security of the whole community. This will not only make more money available to those monks and nuns who need help but will also strengthen the sense of togetherness and responsibility for each other within the Sangha community.

You can support the Lama Yeshe Sangha Fund by

- Making the LYSF the beneficiary of your will
- Making the LYSF the beneficiary of your life insurance policy
- Organizing a fund raising event
- Donating a percentage of the proceeds of a teaching
- Talking to friends and center members about the LYSF

Your contribution will make a difference to the lives of us all. Please contact

Nalanda Monastery
Chateau Rouzegas
Labastide Ste Georges
81500 Lavaur, France.
Tel: + (33) 05 63 58 02 25

Thank you so much.

The Lama Yeshe Wisdom Archive

The LAMA YESHE WISDOM ARCHIVE (LYWA) is the collected works of Lama Thubten Yeshe and Lama Thubten Zopa Rinpoche. Its spiritual director, Lama Zopa Rinpoche, founded the ARCHIVE in 1996 to make available in various ways the teachings it contains. Publication and distribution of free books of edited teachings like this is one of the ways.

Lama Yeshe and Lama Zopa Rinpoche began teaching at Kopan Monastery, Nepal, in 1970. Since then, their teachings have been recorded and transcribed. At present the LYWA contains about 7,000 cassette tapes and approximately 45,000 pages of transcribed teachings on computer disk. Many tapes, mostly teachings by Lama Zopa Rinpoche, remain to be transcribed. As Rinpoche continues to teach, the number of tapes in the ARCHIVE increases accordingly. Most of the transcripts have been neither checked nor edited.

Here at the LYWA we are making every effort to organize the transcription of that which has not yet been transcribed, to edit that which has not yet been edited, and generally to do the many other tasks detailed as follows. In all this, we need your help. Please contact us for more information:

LAMA YESHE WISDOM ARCHIVE
PO Box 356, Weston, MA 02493, USA
Telephone (781) 899-9587; fax (413) 845-9239
info@LamaYeshe.com
www.LamaYeshe.com

THE ARCHIVE TRUST

The work of the LAMA YESHE WISDOM ARCHIVE falls into two categories: archiving and dissemination.

ARCHIVING requires managing the audiotapes of teachings by Lama Yeshe and Lama Zopa Rinpoche that have already been collected, collecting tapes of teachings given but not yet sent to the ARCHIVE, and collecting tapes of Lama Zopa's on-going teachings, talks, advice and so forth as he travels the world for the benefit of all. Tapes are then catalogued and stored safely while being kept accessible for further work.

We organize the transcription of tapes, add the transcripts to the already existent database of teachings, manage this database, have transcripts checked, and make transcripts available to editors or others doing research on or practicing these teachings.

Other archiving activities include working with videotapes and photographs of the Lamas and digitizing ARCHIVE materials.

DISSEMINATION involves making the Lamas' teachings available directly or indirectly through various avenues such as books for free distribution, regular books for the trade, lightly edited transcripts, audio- and videotapes, and articles in Mandala and other magazines, and on our Web site. Irrespective of the method we choose, the teachings require a significant amount of work to prepare them for distribution.

This is just a summary of what we do. The ARCHIVE was established with virtually no seed funding and has developed solely through the kindness of many people, some of whom we have mentioned at the front of this book.

Our further development similarly depends upon the generosity of those who see the benefit and necessity of this work, and we would be extremely grateful for your help.

THE ARCHIVE TRUST has been established to fund the above activities and we hereby appeal to you for your kind support. If you would like to make a contribution to help us with any of the above tasks or to sponsor books for free distribution, please contact us by any of the means shown above.

The LAMA YESHE WISDOM ARCHIVE is a 501(c)(3) tax-deductible, non-profit corporation (ID number 04-3374479) dedicated to the welfare of all sentient beings and totally dependent upon your donations for its continued existence.

Thank you so much for your support. You may contribute by mailing a check, bank draft or money order to our Weston address; by mailing or faxing us your credit card number or by phoning it in; or by transferring funds directly to our bank:

Fleet Bank
ABA routing number 011000138
Account: LYWA 546-81495
SWIFT address: FNBB US 33

THE FOUNDATION FOR THE PRESERVATION OF THE MAHAYANA TRADITION

The Foundation for the Preservation of the Mahayana Tradition (FPMT) is an international organization of Buddhist meditation study and retreat centers, both urban and rural, monasteries, publishing houses, healing centers and other related activities founded in 1975 by Lama Thubten Yeshe and Lama Thubten Zopa Rinpoche. At present, there are more than 150 FPMT activities in twenty-eight countries worldwide.

The FPMT has been established to facilitate the study and practice of Mahayana Buddhism in general and the Tibetan Gelug tradition, founded in the fifteenth century by the great scholar, yogi and saint, Lama Je Tsong Khapa, in particular.

Every three months, the Foundation publishes a magazine, *Mandala*, from its International Office in the United States of America. To subscribe or view back issues, please go to the *Mandala* Web site, www.mandalamagazine.org, or contact:

FPMT
125B La Posta Rd., Taos, NM 87571, USA
Telephone (505) 758-7766; fax (505) 758-7765
fpmtinfo@fpmt.org
www.fpmt.org

Our Web site also offers teachings by His Holiness the Dalai Lama, Lama Yeshe, Lama Zopa Rinpoche and many other highly respected teachers in the tradition, details about the FPMT's educational programs, a complete listing of FPMT centers all over the world and in your area, and links to FPMT centers on the Web, where you will find details of their programs, and other interesting Buddhist and Tibetan home pages.

What to do with Dharma teachings

The Buddhadharma is the true source of happiness for all sentient beings. Books like the one in your hand show you how to put the teachings into practice and integrate them into your life, whereby you get the happiness you seek. Therefore, anything containing Dharma teachings or the names of your teachers is more precious than other material objects and should be treated with respect. To avoid creating the karma of not meeting the Dharma again in future lives, please do not put books (or other holy objects) on the floor or underneath other stuff, step over or sit upon them, or use them for mundane purposes such as propping up wobbly tables. They should be kept in a clean, high place, separate from worldly writings, and wrapped in cloth when being carried around. These are but a few considerations.

Should you need to get rid of Dharma materials, they should not be thrown in the rubbish but burned in a special way. Briefly: do not incinerate such materials with other trash, but alone, and as they burn, recite the mantra OM AH HUM. As the smoke rises, visualize that it pervades all of space, carrying the essence of the Dharma to all sentient beings in the six samsaric realms, purifying their minds, alleviating their suffering, and bringing them all happiness, up to and including enlightenment. Some people might find this practice a bit unusual, but it is given according to tradition. Thank you very much.

Dedication

Through the merit created by preparing, reading, thinking about and sharing this book with others, may all teachers of the Dharma live long and healthy lives, may the Dharma spread throughout the infinite reaches of space, and may all sentient beings quickly attain enlightenment.

In whichever realm, country, area or place this book may be, may there be no war, drought, famine, disease, injury, disharmony or unhappiness, may there be only great prosperity, may everything needed be easily obtained, and may all be guided by only perfectly qualified Dharma teachers, enjoy the happiness of Dharma, have love and compassion for all sentient beings, and only benefit and never harm each other.

LAMA THUBTEN YESHE was born in Tibet in 1935. At the age of six, he entered the great Sera Monastic University, Lhasa, where he studied until 1959, when the Chinese invasion of Tibet forced him into exile in India. Lama Yeshe continued to study and meditate in India until 1967, when, with his chief disciple, Lama Thubten Zopa Rinpoche, he went to Nepal. Two years later he established Kopan Monastery, near Kathmandu, in order to teach Buddhism to Westerners. In 1974, the Lamas began making annual teaching tours to the West, and as a result of these travels a worldwide network of Buddhist teaching and meditation centers—the Foundation for the Preservation of the Mahayana Tradition—began to develop. In 1984, after an intense decade of imparting a wide variety of incredible teachings and establishing one FPMT activity after another, at the age of forty-nine, Lama Yeshe passed away. He was reborn as Osel Hita Torres in Spain in 1985, recognized as the incarnation of Lama Yeshe by His Holiness the Dalai Lama in 1986, and, as the monk Lama Tenzin Osel Rinpoche, is studying for his geshe degree at the reconstituted Sera Monastery in South India. He is sixteen years old. Lama's remarkable story is told in Vicki Mackenzie's book, *Reincarnation: The Boy Lama* (Wisdom Publications, 1996).

Some of Lama Yeshe's teachings have also been published by Wisdom. Books include *Wisdom Energy; Introduction to Tantra; The Tantric Path of Purification;* and *The Bliss of Inner Fire.* Transcripts in print are *Light of Dharma; Life, Death and After Death;* and *Transference of Consciousness at the Time of Death.* Available through FPMT centers or at www.wisdompubs.org. Other teachings may be found on-line at www.LamaYeshe.com.

Lama Yeshe on videotape: *Introduction to Tantra, The Three Principal Aspects of the Path,* and *Offering Tsok to Heruka Vajrasattva.* Available from the LAMA YESHE WISDOM ARCHIVE.

LAMA THUBTEN ZOPA RINPOCHE was born in Thami, Nepal, in 1946. At the age of three he was recognized as the reincarnation of the Lawudo Lama, who had lived nearby at Lawudo, within sight of Rinpoche's Thami home. Rinpoche's own description of his early years may be found in his book, *The Door to Satisfaction* (Wisdom Publications). At the age of ten, Rinpoche went to Tibet and studied and meditated at Domo Geshe Rinpoche's monastery near Pagri, until the Chinese occupation of Tibet in 1959 forced him to forsake Tibet for the safety of Bhutan. Rinpoche then went to the Tibetan refugee camp at Buxa Duar, West Bengal, India, where he met Lama Yeshe, who became his closest teacher. The Lamas went to Nepal in 1967, and over the next few years built Kopan and Lawudo Monasteries. In 1971 Lama Zopa Rinpoche gave the first of his famous annual lam-rim retreat courses, which continue at Kopan to this day. In 1974, with Lama Yeshe, Rinpoche began traveling the world to teach and establish centers of Dharma. When Lama Yeshe passed away in 1984, Rinpoche took over as spiritual head of the FPMT, which has continued to flourish under his peerless leadership. More details of Rinpoche's life and work may be found on the LYWA and FPMT Web sites, www.LamaYeshe.com and www.fpmt.org respectively. In addition to several LYWA books, Rinpoche's other published teachings include *Wisdom Energy* (with Lama Yeshe), *Transforming Problems, Ultimate Healing* and a number of transcripts and practice booklets.